Brett Parks tells an inspiring story of freedom, fear, fight, and faith. He joined the Navy out of a sense of patriotism and gratitude for the freedom he enjoyed as an American citizen in a post 9/11 society. Then, in a moment of genuine fear, he chose not to run, but to chase, and in the midst of defending another, he was brutally shot, critically wounded, and ultimately left for dead. As days turned to weeks, he chose to fight for his life--a decision made out of faith for the very life he knew he was called to live and the message he was chosen to deliver. Brett is a tribute to his country, to his community, and to his faith.

—Kate Ziegler
United States Olympic Team (2008, 2012)

There is a country song that says "Live Like You're Dying." The only thing more inspirational would be to LIVE after you come as close to death as you possibly could. How would our lives be different? Do we have to actually come face to face with death or can we learn from someone who has? Brett LIVED to tell the story of what it's like, you have the opportunity to have the same changed life without the near death experience. Read the book. Put yourself in his shoes and LIVE like you have never LIVED before!

—Caz McCaslin
President Upward Sports

BRETT PARKS
MIRACLE MAN

A BULLET THAT IGNITED
A PURPOSE–FILLED LIFE

AMBASSADOR INTERNATIONAL
GREENVILLE, SOUTH CAROLINA & BELFAST, NORTHERN IRELAND

www.ambassador-international.com

Miracle Man:
A Bullet that Ignited a Purpose-Filled Life

ISBN: 978-1-62020-514-3
eISBN: 978-1-62020-420-7

Cover Design & Page Layout by Hannah Nichols
eBook Conversion by Anna Riebe Raats

AMBASSADOR INTERNATIONAL
Emerald House
427 Wade Hampton Blvd.
Greenville, SC 29609, USA
www.ambassador-international.com

AMBASSADOR BOOKS
The Mount
2 Woodstock Link
Belfast, BT6 8DD, Northern Ireland, UK
www.ambassadormedia.co.uk

The colophon is a trademark of Ambassador

For my Jason and Stella, so they know where their daddy has been.

ACKNOWLEDGEMENTS

First and foremost, I'd like to thank my Lord and Savior, Jesus Christ, for, if not for Him, these events are for nothing.

My rock and my heart, Susan.

My children, Jason and Stella, for igniting the spark of motivation that kept me fighting for my next breath.

Mom (Greta Parks-Mealey)

Dad (Brian Parks)

Derek and Ginger Parks

Courtney and Tim Lemkie

Kenton and Diane Lynn

John and Denise Jeselnik

"Mema" and "G'dad" (Jack and Greta Brasington)

Sam and Jimmie Davis

Brian, Catlin, and Sean Mealey

Nancy Brasington, Hunter, and Brooke Reid

Chris and Cantillon Eiler and Family

Ken Mick and the Argyle Church of Christ Family

Bill White and the Christ Journey Family (University Baptist Church)

Greg and Kay Gackle

Geoff and Janeen Gackle

Chris and Krista Farrington

Matt and Reina McDonald

Kathy and Brian Gilmore

Jack (Jackie Boy) and Kimberly Brasington

Jonathan Pabalate

Brian and Kim Rahal

Chris and Susan Kahn

Robbie and Eileen Mateu

Anthony Fadelle

Raquel Morales

Garrett Hundley

Shawn Eckert

Clint Mason

Mark Mason

Garella Family

Owen Salfen

Paul Rodgers

Tracy Hejemenowski

Tiffany Wilson

Tony Randolph

Val and Traci Janshulz

Carolina Christian Writers Conference

Naval Hospital Jacksonville

My physical Therapists, Gerry Dumlao and Theresa Poblete, Luann Dewaart, Mylyn Shelvy

MWR Fitness Center- NAS JAX

United States Navy

VP-30, NAS JAX

Navy Safe Harbor

Wounded Warrior Project- Jack and Andrew

Operation Outdoor Freedom

Florida Forestry Department

J.T. Townsend Foundation

The Blood Alliance

Patriot Service Dogs

Caringbridge.org

USO

The Zitello family

Joe Mira

John and Rochelle Chiocca

Leslie Stobbe

Kumasi Aaron

Kristen Sell

Geoff and the Hanger Clinic

Governor Rick Scott

Mayor Alvin Brown

Jacksonville City Council

James A. Haley Veterans Hospital

Roman, Kerri and Kerry (V.A. Hospital Therapists)

Lt. Sandra Lockett

Lt. Chet Frith

Dr. Dobertene

"Doc" Brown

U.F. Health/Shands Hospital- Jacksonville: Trauma One

Dr. Andrew Kerwin

Dr. Eric Roberts

Dr. Chester Royals

Dr. Hud Berrey

Dr. James Dennis

Dr. James

Heather Wood Calfee

Coach Raulson and the Providence Football Team

Ambassador International

CONTENTS

CHAPTER 1

HOW IT ALL BEGAN

Before I formed you in the womb, I knew you, before you were born I set you apart.

~ Jeremiah 1:5 NIV

THE LEAVES IN OCTOBER ARE usually the colors of autumn, crackling in the cool breeze, oranges and browns silhouetting the blue sky, with purple and orange clouds showing signs of dusk. But in this particular season and in this Florida town, the leaves are still green and the breeze is still warm when it brushes your cheek. Only an hour north, in Georgia, do you truly feel the effects of shorter days as people carve their pumpkins and children grow ever more excited as Halloween draws near.

October 17, 2012 started as any other day for me. Just like every day, I would wake up, take my son to daycare, go to work for the United States Navy, pick my son up, take him home to my wife, and go to lead a fitness training session. But this day was different.

Coming in contact with a monster face to face was not expected at least until October 31st. As the sun was preparing for its slumber, a creature of the ugliest kind did its worst on me. A bullet ripped through my abdomen, traveled down my body, severed my vena cava, and sent me crumbling to the ground in a lonely parking lot. The warm concrete comforted me as my body ran cold, and I began to fade away into the great unknown. Fear ran through my heart as I thought of my unborn daughter. *What kind of woman will she grow up to be without her daddy to love her? Who will walk her down the aisle on her wedding day? My son. What kind of legacy did I leave for him to follow? My wife. She loves me and will miss me for the rest of her life.* The emotional pain was as unbearable as the physical pain, but both began to fade as the seconds turned to minutes. *I'm in shock; I'm dying. This cannot happen. The evil one cannot win. He sent death after me. He's been roaming throughout the earth, and now he's found me.*

A dark shadow surrounded me as the warm breeze turned to a damp chill. I opened my eyes to see a young woman kneeling close by. She never touched me. She only rocked and prayed with her hand outstretched toward me. As my pleading eyes met hers, she reassured me through a gaze, "You are going to be okay." Was I hallucinating from the shock, or was she sent to plead for my life?

The battle raged between life and death. Death could taste the victory as he stared into my eyes. I sensed a smirk spread across his contorted face as my heartbeat slowed and my hands turned to ice.

One of us is going to blink, and it cannot be me. It must not be me. I have everything to live for.

I had heard the cries for help. I answered the call. But was it worth it? You never know how hard you'll cling to life until you're losing it. Movies make death look so beautiful, so romantic. As the blood poured out of my abdomen and trickled out of the corners of my mouth, my final moments were anything but beautiful. Screams of agonizing pain echoed throughout the condo buildings as my exploded colon seeped feces onto my organs, making certain if the bullet didn't kill me, septic poisoning would.

Every breath is laborious. Every second is a fight for survival. *If I can only make it to the hospital, everything will be okay. If I can just stay awake until the paramedics get here, I'll be safe. If I can just keep on breathing; I need to keep on breathing. Why is it so cold now? Why am I shivering? The sky looks so beautiful. The green leaves against the blue, orange, and purple colored sky is awe inspiring. I wish Susie could be here right now. I'd love to share this sunset with her; my last sunset.*

My blood tastes horrible. I want to spit it out, but I don't want to die with my face resting in my blood and saliva. The chill in my bone creeps in as I see the first signs of police lights in the distance. I'm shivering harder now. *Why am I so cold? I was hot ten minutes ago. Did the temperature drop that much in such little time? Oh no, my blood. I'm losing too much blood. I'm bleeding out. Time is my enemy, and it's winning.*

How did I get here, I ask myself while trying to trick my body into thinking everything is going to be okay. This must be the time when your life flashes before your eyes. The word *flash* is an inappropriate term as my thoughts lazily stroll through the forefront of my mind. What do I remember? I need to keep my mind busy. Take my mind off the pain. *My childhood—I remember my childhood.*

I remember waking up early on sticky Miami Saturday mornings with my brother to watch Hulk Hogan on the World Wrestling Federation's show "WWF Superstars." I remember being in awe of the size and strength of the Hulkster as he stood up against injustice and protected the little man. It was then that I fell in love with fitness. I knew if I trained hard, said my prayers, and ate my vitamins, I would one day be strong enough to stand up for injustice and protect the little man as well. I guess I should thank Mr. Hogan for influencing me at such a young age. If not for him, I wouldn't be lying here in crippling pain right now. But then again, his influencing me to train hard might just save my life.

With the help of my parents kicking me out of the house all weekend to keep me away from the "idiot box" (as my dad called the TV), I learned how to inadvertently train my body by bike riding, freeze tag, kick the can, and challenging neighborhood kids (or dogs) to wrestling matches. I lost more than I won, but that never stopped me from continuing to challenge those who had just licked me in battle.

I remember one wrestling match like it was yesterday: As I was building a fort in a fresh trash pile I had recently discovered (that's right, I was a dirty child), I was challenged to a wrestling match by two girls who lived down the street. Amused by this, I accepted their challenge as I walked to the nearest yard and blocked off a ring with my shoes, my shirt, and a tree. I wasn't going to miss the trash pile. It was midday, and the heap was beginning to smell ripe in the July sun. Besides, it wasn't going anywhere for a few days.

Now, there's only one thing easier than beating two girls in a fight and that's beating one girl in a fight—or so I thought. Apparently, these girls didn't know the rules of professional wrestling because all they did was pull hair, scratch, kick, and bite. On second thought, maybe they did know the rules. Now, let me tell you, I was going to kick those girls' rear ends from Miami all the way to Atlanta! I was going to dominate! But I wasn't ready. And as I was in the process of summoning the power of the Hulkster, I was ambushed! As one girl grabbed the back of my mullet and yanked me to the ground, the other began stomping my pliable ribs till I heard a crack. Face down on the grassy ring, I felt a clump of blonde hair tickling my nose. About four minutes later, I ran home crying. I didn't even grab my shoes and shirt. There was no time. I had to retreat. I just got whooped by girls, and it hurt both my ego and my body. I didn't have any broken ribs, but they were tender for a while. But that day didn't stop me from "wrasslin';" it just made me work harder. I knew that the pain of losing hurt far worse than the pain of pushing your body to become the best it could be. Rest assured, when those two girls challenged me to another fight a few days later, I did what any smart man would do; I ran as fast as I could.

My brother, Derek, and I as kids

Derek was born on October 3, 1975. He was just three years older than I was, but to me it felt like a life-time. Normally, older brothers don't want their kid brothers hanging around. The older brother gets embarrassed and doesn't include his younger brother in any of the fun stuff that his friends are get-ting into. That couldn't be said about Derek. My brother included me in everything he did. It didn't matter if he was going out with his friends or listening to music in his room. It was always, "Come on, Bwett [Brett]." Or, "Hey, Bwett, let's wide [ride] our bikes to the woks [rocks]." Yes, his speech was a bit off. I couldn't believe my big brother wanted little me around. As his friends' younger brothers' were left staring out the window as the big boys rode their bikes into the sunset, I was never on the inside looking out. I was riding into the sunset with the big guys.

He, being three years stronger than I, made me have to work three times as hard to keep up with him. I had to ride much farther and harder than I might otherwise be expected to because I didn't want to lose favor with him. I held my own, but he was smart enough to throw me a bone here and there to keep my morale up.

I remember Derek and I cut a championship wrestling belt out of an old cardboard box. We wrestled in the TV room more times than I could count. His finishing move was the "figure four." Let me tell you, my shins took a beating. My finishing move was the "off the couch flying elbow" which I only got to do once or twice. Being the older, stronger boy, Derek had his way with me in the "ring," but every so often, he would let me win. He always knew when I was about to break. All it would take from him was a victory or a pat on the back, and I was back in the game. He still knows this about me today.

One time, Derek put me in the sleeper hold, courtesy of Jake "The Snake" Roberts. Unlike in the professional wrestling community, my brother really put me to sleep. He sunk a deep sleeper hold that cuts off circulation to the brain, causing a person to go unconscious. Once I was asleep, Derek released the hold. Unfortunately for me, we were standing. When he let go of my limp body, I fell, face first, onto the tile floor.

In a panic, Derek flipped me over to my back to see that not only was my mouth bleeding from the fall, but he also busted a blood vessel in my eye, causing blood to trickle down my face. This gave the effect that I was crying blood. This would have looked pretty cool if I hadn't been the guy bleeding. Needless to say, Derek thought he killed me . . . until I woke up crying. This was the first time I remember tasting my own blood.

Courtney is our little princess, being the only girl in the family with two older brothers. (She may kill me for calling her a princess.) I was five years older than my little sister. As you might guess, Courtney and I didn't get along. As a matter of fact, we hated each other's guts. You would think that I would have treated her like a princess and she would have thought I did no wrong, but I treated her like a toad, and the infallibility nod went to Derek, who was eight years older than she was. When she went off to college, we finally began respecting each other. Since those dark times and a lot of maturing on both parts, I can honestly say she is one of my best friends.

I remember I used to go into my mother's room late at night when my sister was watching TV with Mom. I would recite the entire movie "Ace Ventura: Pet Detective" with facial expressions and physical comedy included. I could make my sister laugh harder than anybody. Deep down we really loved each other, but I think my comical moments prevented her murdering me in my sleep. I'm mostly kidding, but my comedy did help.

Brian, better known as Dad, was very instrumental in my life. My earliest memories of him were wrestling with him right before dinner. This was also some of my fondest memories until sometime after high school. I remember Hank Williams Jr. playing in the background as I wrestled with Dad in the living room as Mom made the finishing touches on the family meal, its scent filling the room. My dad never let me beat him before dinner, especially on the nights he knew we were eating spinach. He knew I was a Popeye fan, so he would beat me up until my mom called us for dinner. My dad would say I better eat my spinach if I had a chance of taking him on. I knew the game he was playing. So I'd run to the dinner table and eat as much spinach as I could to get as strong as I could. Then, like clockwork, after dinner we would have another match, and I would take him to the cleaners! He got me to eat my vegetables—good strategy for a parent. But he did more than trick me to eat what I hated; he put me on track to see that smart eating equals stronger bones and stronger muscles.

The word on the street was that Greta (my mom) had been the fastest girl in her high school. She was an incredible athlete as well as having incredible beauty. One of my earliest memories of my mom was racing her down the street in our neighborhood. We'd line up, both barefoot, and she'd say, "On your mark, get set, GO!" And like a shot out of a cannon, she would be gone! She would beat both my brother and I for years. I always got mad at her and begged her to let me win, but her response was always the same, "No way! I'll always run my fastest because one day you're gonna beat me, and after that day, I'll never beat you again." So I ran sprints and tried to get faster every day to beat her, and one day I did. Moms are usually right. She never beat me in a race again.

From the early years with my family to junior high school, I really honed in on my athletic skills. I was even awarded my school's "Most Athletic" award. As I walked up the driveway one day when I was in eighth grade, I couldn't believe my eyes. My dream had come true. Right there in my very own garage was top of the line bench press equipment and dumbbells. When I say "Top of the line," I really mean

"Top of the line that we could afford." My dad met me in the driveway and said, "Go change your clothes. We're gonna work out." He taught me the benefits of lifting weights and using proper form to prevent injuries. He also taught me to do at least one more rep when I feel like I can't do another. He called it the "strength rep."

After this first workout with my dad, I was hooked. I loved lifting weights! The feeling I felt—and still feel—after a good workout is addictive. I also noticed that it was helping me be more athletic. I was fast before, but I became faster. I was quick before, but weights made me quicker. Once I saw the changes lifting weights offered me, you couldn't keep me out of the weight room. Even in college, after our football workout, I'd walk over to the student weight room and do another workout. I didn't have a set goal; I just knew that I loved lifting weights. Little did I know lifting weights would later save my life.

CHAPTER 2

CHANGE OF HEART

"The only necessary for the triumph of evil is for
good men to do nothing."

~ Edmund Burke

MY FRESHMAN YEAR IN JUNIOR high wasn't the best year of my life. There were a number of things that caused me problems. The school building was a two story, windowless structure that was built like a maze. Every corner you turned would look exactly like the hall you just left. So, if you got turned around, you were lost. And since you had only five minutes to get to your next class, one mix up meant you'd be late and receive after-school detention. The school seemed to be built more like a correctional facility than an educational one, with only a few tiny windows in the building, ten foot tall fences, and security guards armed with brick-like walkie-talkies around every corner. After a long day in the school that I later labeled "The Compound," my eyes would hurt when I walked out into the sun.

Not only was the compound unbearable, but my hormones were messing with me. As we all know, at a certain age, we go through a hormone change that society calls puberty. I called it hell. When I was growing up, most kids would go through puberty at twelve or thirteen years old (at least boys did). Of course, you had your early bloomers and your late bloomers as well. I was a very late bloomer. I felt like I went through puberty from thirteen till age sixteen. So basically, my entire junior high experience was full of voice cracking, pimple popping, and hair growing in places I didn't think possible. One of my biggest fears at the time was of the teacher calling me up to her desk or making me walk up to the chalk board to figure out an equation. It wasn't the humiliation of not knowing how to solve the particular math problem (not knowing it was a given); it was what was going on with my anatomy that terrified me. Not fun. I actually went as far as to think of Jesus when I had a certain flare up (I'm trying to keep it PG here). Then I had to deal with this funny feeling I'd get when a girl would sit next to me in class. I always had crushes on girls, all the way back to first grade, but this was an entirely different feeling all together. Let's not forget Hurricane Andrew, which gave me my first feeling of thinking I was actually going to die. Hurricanes were just hurricanes down in Miami. They were never a big deal, until Andrew came rolling into town. Then to top it all off, my parents began going through a divorce. There is no pain like a broken heart, and that was my first bout with it. It wouldn't be my last. Closing the book on that chapter of my life couldn't have come sooner. I couldn't have been happier to move on to senior high school.

The summer between my freshman year and sophomore year, I grew about three inches and put on about fifteen pounds. Thanks to my dad teaching me the fundamentals of lifting weights, I had a strong foundation and knowledge of working out. I was still relatively weak entering an actual weight room, but my football coach put me on a program that helped me put on some pounds as well as increase my speed, quickness, and strength.

Life was looking up. I was one of the better wide receivers in Dade County (South Florida), as well as being one of the leaders on my football team. I was one of the spiritual leaders, as well as a leader on the field. Our football team had a sort of spiritual awakening when my best friend (Chris) and I were seniors. Every day, before practice, we would all join hands in a circle and pray together. It gave our team a closeness that we never had at Palmetto. Unfortunately, the closeness didn't transfer to wins on the field. We ended up with six wins and five losses, though our cheerleaders went on to win the national championship for competitive cheering. I felt humiliated, but the good news is that, years later, I ended up marrying one of those cheerleaders. Who's the national champ now?

I was very involved in my church, University Baptist, and was the president of the Fellowship of Christian Athletes (FCA) at my school. By the time I graduated from high school, I was a two-time "Outstanding Wide Receiver" and had received a football

My sister, Courtney, and I during my senior year

scholarship to Carson Newman College (Jefferson City, TN). Things were looking up for me, at least on the athletic field. Academically, I was average at best.

I was never pushed in the classroom the way that I was pushed on the football field. In athletics, be it baseball, basketball, or my beloved football, I was taught to be perfect. I was taught that if you strive for perfection and you fall short, the least you would be is great. I was taught how to run a perfect route, how to position my feet when catching a fly ball, and how to have perfect execution when performing a hang clean. Everything was focused on and critiqued by coaches that I loved and respected. In the classroom, I was just a number. I wrote a bunch of nonsense as answers on my tests, but it didn't really matter since my teachers didn't read the answers anyway. I tricked my teachers, but, worst of all, I cheated myself.

About two months before I graduated, I witnessed an incident that changed my life. You know that kid in school who wears a backpack two times his size and packs all his books in it? The backpack being so heavy that he has to lean forward when he walks so his tiny frame won't fall back from the weight of the books? I'm sure there's a kid like that in every school; you may have even been that kid, which means you wouldn't have been in any of my classes. You probably were in all AP classes and earned straight A's. There was a kid like that in my school. I'll call him Jake to protect the innocent. I remember his face vividly. I used to pass him in the halls every day. We weren't friends, but I knew who Jake was and shot him a nod when we passed. I always remembered what my mother told me when I was young. She said, "Always be friendly to everybody, especially the little guy, because you never know what life may bring your way. You may see that person again someday."

One day, as the final bell rang to bring an end to the dismal school day, I grabbed my books and walked out of my classroom like

I did every day. Down the hall, I noticed Jake in front of me, walk-ing urgently toward the parking lot, heavy backpack and all. There was nothing strange about this because he always walked with a pur-pose. Fifteen yards ahead of us were a group of guys standing around and looking like they were up to no good. I kept walking in my casual manner, and Jake, in his sense of urgency walk, was furthering the gap between him and me and closing the gap between him and the suspicious group of guys. What I witnessed next has haunted me to this day and will continue to haunt me.

As Jake was about to pass the group of guys, one of them turned and hit him right in the face with such force that Jake flew out of his shoes and hit the fence about four feet to his left. You probably think I'm exaggerating, but I tell you the truth: Jake flew, and his shoes stayed right where he left them.

My being one of the star football players and the president of FCA surely gives you a heroic picture of what happened next. I ran to Jake and checked on him while I yelled at the group of guys for being a bunch of cowards, even going as far as to chase down the kid that knocked him out and held him until help got there.

I'm sad to report that's not what really happened. After Jake was hit, the group of guys laughed and ran. I walked toward Jake, see-ing him semi-conscious while trying to locate his books and pull them toward him, but I kept walking. I practically stepped right over him. The only coward that day was me, and I knew it. Not even an hour passed before I started feeling guilty. I thought about Jake all the time. At night, when I closed my eyes, I would see Jake on the ground, in a confused state, needing a helping hand. But all I did was walk by. The memory of that day continues to torment me. I wish I could go back. I wish I'd had the heart to stand up for what was right. I wish I'd hurried to his side and told him to just lie still and then comforted him until help arrived. I wish I could get a do-over, but I can't. I have to live with that the rest of my life.

That night, while lying in bed, I made a promise to myself and the Lord. I promised that I'd never walk by someone in danger again. If someone was in need, I would stop and do all that I could. Since that day, the Lord has held me to my promise, and He's given me opportunities to prove it as well. Be it helping a car crash victim on I-95 or coming to someone's rescue during a mugging in New York City, I wasn't going to pass on by. Never again would I turn the other way, no matter what the cost. I had no idea the cost would be great.

CHAPTER 3

ANCHORS AWEIGH

"I can imagine no more rewarding a career. And any man who may be asked in this century what he did to make his life worthwhile, I think can respond with a good deal of pride and satisfaction: 'I served in the United States Navy.'"

~ John Fitzgerald Kennedy

ON OCTOBER 13, 1775, THE Continental Congress passed a resolution creating what we know today as the United States Navy. Two hundred thirty-three years later, on the night of November 17, 2008, I stepped off a bus in freezing Great Lakes, Illinois. Just like every recruit who steps off the bus for the first time, I was wondering what the heck I had gotten myself into. At that moment, most of us thought that we had made a grave mistake, giving our lives to the United States government for the next four to six years. So how'd I get myself into this pickle?

Rewind a few years to September 11, 2001. That particular day changed America and the world as we knew it. A couple of days later, my brother called me, and we seriously considered enlisting in the Marines. We talked a great deal about it but, in time, our emotions

settled a bit, and he realized that he couldn't leave his family or career. However, enlisting wasn't too farfetched for me; I was twenty-
something and single. I continued to coach football at my high
school alma mater and softball at Westminster Christian School, and
later I moved to New York City. In the city, I passed by the recruiting station almost every day in Times Square and would think about
enlisting. To tell you the truth, the only thing that kept me from
walking through those doors was my mother's voice, threatening me
if I ever enlisted. My mother's little voice in the back of my head
worked from my senior year of high school until February of 2008. I
wound up living in Spartanburg, South Carolina. My townhouse was
only a mile away from my brother and his family. I had about four
part-time jobs and was still struggling to pay bills and make rent. You
would think that being a bus driver, a computer lab teacher, a softball
coach, and a lifeguard would pay more than they do, but I still struggled. As I was working one day, I received a text from one of my best
friends, Matt. The only thing he asked in the text was if I wanted to
join the reserves with him. Without hesitation, I texted back, "Sure."
Matt was pretty much in the same position I was in. He was a few
years younger and was also finding it hard to make ends meet. Later
that day, we talked about what would be the best military branch for
the reserves. We eventually settled with the Air Force. Not only did
the Air Force have the highest ASVAB (a test you take to determine
if you are "smart" enough to enlist in a particular branch) requirements of all military branches, but it also has the highest budget for
morale purposes. For example, beautiful golf courses and top of the
line workout facilities.

At this time, Matt was living down in Miami, and I was in South Carolina. So we arranged a time for him to come up so we could go to the recruiter's station to ask questions and, eventually, enlist together. Matt drove up and stayed with me for about five days, each day going to the Air Force recruiter's station. Each day it was closed. Apparently, it was really good to be in the Air Force, because they were NEVER there, even on weekdays! In most strip malls or regular malls, where you see one branch of the military recruiting station, you see all of them. Well, the last day of Matt's visit, we made one last effort to get into Air Force's door so we could ask a few questions. Not surprisingly, it was closed. As we were standing there, dogging out the Air Force and assuming they were on a golf course somewhere, a sailor stepped out of the Navy recruiting station located right next door. He was standing there in his crisp white uniform and black shoes polished so well that I could see my reflection looking back at me. He asked if he could help us. I, rather dismissively, told him that we weren't looking for Navy. He asked if we wanted to come in and talk to him about the military. He told us that he could answer any questions we had. Well, he was good. After about thirty minutes, both Matt and I signed a letter of intent to enlist in the United States Navy. Our original plan to enlist as reservists in the Air Force went right out the door! We both blew away the ASVAB test requirements and were just waiting for our recruiter to get the paperwork together so we could go down to Columbia, South Carolina, to take the oath that less than one percent of Americans ever take:

> I, (your name), do solemnly swear that I will support and
> defend the Constitution of the United States against all en-
> emies, foreign and domestic; that I will bear true faith and

allegiance to the same; and I will obey the orders of the president of the United States and the orders of the officers appointed over me, according to regulations and the military code of justice. So help me God.

Unfortunately, only one of us took that oath a few weeks later. Our recruiter had messed up Matt's paperwork; only I was allowed to enlist. Matt could still enlist, but it would have been at a later date, and we couldn't expect to be in boot camp at the same time. Looking back, I can guarantee that we wouldn't have been in the same boot camp class. There would have been a good chance that I would never even see Matt again, unless, of course, we went on leave at the same time.

My Navy Portrait

I decided on enlisting as a Search and Rescue swimmer. I briefly considered enlisting as a Navy SEAL—until I read a chapter of Marcus Luttrell's book *Lone Survivor*, where it talks about SEAL training. Reading his description of the grueling training regiment made me want to take a nap. It exhausted me, and I was just sitting on the couch. I also wanted a job that would help people in a more direct way. When someone's in the ocean drowning, there seems to be no hope for their survival. For the victim, hopelessness and pain sets in as the reality of the circumstance sinks in. What a great feeling it would be to be his rescuer, to fill the victim with the hope that he lost just moments before. To save life is far more rewarding than to take life. I hadn't forgotten the promise I made to God my senior year in high school.

This is how I feel about telling people about Jesus Christ and His love for us. Here we are, drowning in this ocean of darkness and emptiness.

Hopelessness sets in as we start to sink into the depths. That's when our Lord reaches out and snatches us from the depths, filling us back up with a new hope and a new reality. Rescue swimming was the job for me.

So there I was, in the middle of the night, being herded into a building with all the other poor saps who decided that the military was the right fit for them. I've never heard so much screaming and belittling in my life as I did in those few minutes of marching out of the frigid Illinois wind into the even colder hallway of recruit row. To call what we were doing "marching" is an insult to every marine and soldier/sailor who has spent hours upon hours marching. Stumbling is more of an accurate description of what we were doing. About a hundred of us from all over the country "toed the line" on each side of the hallway while being "encouraged" by RDC (Recruit Division Commander), the Navy's equivalent of drill sergeants. Out of nowhere, an eerie silence overcame the once deafening hallway. The RDCs slivered back into the holes where they came from, and the senior chief walked out into the middle of the hall. It was almost like everybody broke character and became real. Calmly and tenderly, the senior chief thanked us for deciding to enlist in a time of war. He went on to say that less than one percent of the country answers the call and even less during a time of war. He said that he enlisted during peace time, and he probably wouldn't have had enough courage to enlist during a time of war. Senior chief went on to tell us that the first couple weeks of boot camp were going to be rough but to just keep hanging on because it would get better. He then said that he knew that we were probably all regretting the decision we made to enlist, but we made the right choice. He commended us for it. Any doubts that most of us had were cast out after the man's pep talk. We answered the call, and we were just thanked for it.

As suddenly as the senior chief came into our lives, he left, and the RDCs crept from the shadows and started their charade once more. Just as senior told us, the next few weeks were tough as we learned how to strip away our civilian ways and conform to the military mold. It wasn't tough in the physical standpoint, but the mental. In the military, there is no room for personalities and/or opinions. Three hundred years of military tradition isn't going to change because you feel like waking up at eight o'clock. Nope! If you're not following orders at four-thirty in the morning, fire and brimstone will rain down on you.

This was especially hard for me, not because I liked my beauty rest (which I did), but because I enlisted at twenty-nine years of age. Most of these kids go straight from high school into the military. They basically trade their parents in for a new set of authority figures. But I'd been in the civilian world and away from my parents for eleven years. I was my own person and much more mature than most of my "shipmates." Okay, maybe not much more, but I'd been around the block a couple times. Of course, during my twelve weeks of boot camp life, I acquired the nickname Dad because of my age. I even taught one of my guys how to shave. Here was an eighteen-year-old young man who had never been taught how to shave his face. I didn't know his history, but his father failed him. I was very happy to teach him the steps of shaving that my dad taught me.

I became a leader within the barracks because of my strength and training techniques. After lights out, I would jump out of my bunk and perform numerous sets of push-ups, sit-ups, flutter kicks, and crab walks before calling it a day. After a while, I had about ten guys working out with me.

I remember one guy in particular who was a body builder in the civilian world. He was huge! He reminded me of Arnold Schwarzenegger. He was maybe a foot shorter than Arnold but had the same build. I admired his commitment in the weight room, the commitment it takes to sculpt the kind of body he had, as I do all body builders. It seems that a body builder would look at my work-out routine and laugh, but when he worked out with me, he was hurting. When I did flutter kicks with him, we'd agree on doing a hundred four-count kicks and then take a forty-five second rest and start again. Well, I was never satisfied with our one-hundred goal, so when we'd get to a hundred, I'd keep going and tell him that we were going to a hundred fifteen or a hundred twenty-five. He would continue with me, of course, but he would be cursing me out the whole time. It was so funny that sometimes I could barely finish because I was laughing so hard.

Because we weren't satisfied with the physical training that boot camp offered us, and we stayed up late at night, pushing our bodies to the max, we ended up winning the Captain's Cup (a physical competition between all the classes) that consisted of push-ups, sit-ups, pull ups, running, etc. We even beat the special ops barracks (SEALs, EODs, and Navy Divers). I graduated boot camp in great physical condition, ready to take on the physically demanding Aircrew School and after, the Rescue Swimming School located back in my home state of sunny Florida!

Aircrew, in the Navy, is a special program. We weren't as high up as the SEALs, but we were a level higher than the regular Navy. Because of the aircrew rate, flying over enemy territory with the possibility of being shot down, we had to be in peak condition. If we were shot down behind enemy lines, we would need to be strong and fast to evade capture in hostile territory.

I showed up at NAS Pensacola (Florida) at eleven-thirty at night, exhausted and ready to lie back and re-energize after twelve weeks of boot camp living. My hope of relaxation was squashed as soon as I set foot in the Aircrew Candidate School's quarterdeck. I thought boot camp was bad, but it was a cake walk compared to the hell that Aircrew Candidate School comprised of. Daily room inspections, uniform perfection inspections, and intense two-a-day physical training sessions were just a small part of my experience at Aircrew School.

The physical training wasn't too hard for me. I've been training with the kind of workouts that was demanded of us my whole life, so my body could adapt to the physical stress fairly easy. My past training also allowed me to push a little harder during the pt sessions, which allowed me to stand out and be a leader in the school. The only difficult thing for me in Aircrew School, as well as in boot camp, was the mental aspect of training. It's one thing to put maximum stress on your body to better improve your fitness level and give yourself an edge physically, but it's another thing to push your body to the max while a guy who has half the physical capacity as you is yelling in your ear.

Don't get me wrong—I think a person motivating you to do one or two more reps is a good thing, but these petty officers were belittling us from the first rep to the last. Hazing was banned by the time I enlisted, so I guess it was their way of hazing.

I have always had a problem with the mental aspect. I never believed that a guy of my age and maturity should be treated like a kindergartner unless, of course, the guy acted like a kindergartner. If one of those petty officers wanted something done, all they had to do was ask me; I would have done it a hundred percent. That's how I was built. But a thirty-year-old being treated the same as a jacked-up eighteen-year-old just shows that there is a lack of natural leaders in the learning phase in training.

In fitness, and even in the business world, one size never fits all when it comes to motivation. I remember vividly an RDC in boot camp pulling me aside in the mess hall and whispering something in my ear that was so offensive that were I to see him on the street, I probably would have knocked him into next week. But, lucky for me, I had my Lord to fall back on in times like that. More like lucky for him. When the petty officers were yelling at me and belittling me for whatever they supposedly caught me doing or not doing, I would think of Jesus and how He was beaten, bruised, and belittled for claiming to be the King of kings. Well, just like Jesus' accusers, the joke was on them. All the petty officers knew that not only was I in better shape than they were, but I also had the leadership qualities that they lacked, and it showed.

I never sought out a leadership role in Aircrew School, but when you're prepared, both physically and mentally, and the Lord is standing in your corner, people gravitate toward you. I never really had to tell people that I was a Christian, but they saw something different about me: a light in the dark place called Aircrew School and, later, Rescue Swimming School.

A leader I became, rather reluctantly. I became a duty section leader and a class leader in both Aircrew School and Rescue Swimming School. I say reluctantly because I just wanted to keep my head down and get through all the schooling. I didn't want to be held accountable for twenty-five kids who had the mentality that they had nothing to lose. I didn't even want the instructors to know my name. But, if you excel in your career choice, you're going to stand out. Oops.

Aircrew Candidate School came and went in a blur. I was in top physical condition and ready to take on my next school by storm. Rescue Swimming School was in for a treat. Brett Parks was about to step onto the quarterdeck and grace them all with his presence, so, "You're welcome." Or so I thought.

Just as I was about to lead my shipmates into the RSS building, we were bombarded by a slew of petty officers who were as in shape, if not in better shape, than me. I'd met my match, and for the first time in my naval adventure, I felt a shroud of panic coming over me.

After the smoke cleared, my instincts took over and it was business as usual. I excelled in the physical training and was even acing my first aid tests. One of the more challenging parts of our workouts was the beach runs. Pensacola, Florida, is known for some of the most beautiful beaches in the nation. The sand is so fine and deep that when you walk on it, it's like walking on fluffy clouds that fall into the crystal clear waters of the Gulf of Mexico. But, when you are running across it, it's like running in hummus. After about twenty yards, my thighs burned like fire. I don't have muscular legs.

Back then, my girlfriend at the time (who later became my wife) would call me "chicken" because of my chicken legs. I was going to have to put some muscle on those toothpicks quick, or I was never going to make it. Going through Rescue Swimming School in the scorching Florida panhandle in June didn't help either. Not only would I have another mile to run in that fine sand that I liked to call "the mouse trap" (because even though it looks so innocent, it'll kill you in the end), but I had to catch my breath in the heat, which was like breathing through a straw.

I perform much better in heat than in cold. I was raised in the tropics where heat and humidity on Christmas Day was the norm. If it fell below seventy degrees outside, out came the snow jacket!

I thought that the swimming portion of RSS would be a challenge for me, but it ended up being fairly easy. Although I was raised in Miami and trained in the water before going to boot camp, I still felt that I would be the most vulnerable in the water. I was surprised to see that I was one of the fastest in my class. That was a huge morale booster for me. I felt that I would be graduating in four weeks time as the "Honor Grad" (the student who had no failures and who the instructors deemed superior among the other students). Unfortunately, my plans were interrupted by technique failure in the water.

In the third week of school, we had to perform three rescue attempts on a drowning swimmer three different ways. The first two rescue techniques were executed to perfection for me, but the third one was the most difficult. We had to swim backwards into the drowning swimmer, and he was supposed to grab us from behind. The rescue swimmer then had to take the swimmer under the water, break the hold, and, while maintaining positive control of the swimmer, position himself behind him, secure him in the rescue hold, resurface, and swim him to safety. Well, I executed every step flawlessly with the exception of one thing. I was told by the RSS instructor that when I positioned myself behind the swimmer, I maintained positive control of him, but there was too much water between the swimmer and me, whatever that meant. So I failed on a technicality. . . twice. I was allowed to take a retest and failed for the same reason. I later found out that the RSS instructors would place bets on the students to predict who will make it through and who will drop out or be dropped from the school. The instructor testing me may have been one of the guys who bet against me. But, the bottom line was that I should have executed that rescue to perfection, but I didn't.

I was rolled out of class and put into student hold until the next class started a few weeks later. This was a concern for me because of all the weight I was losing. In Aircrew School and Rescue Swimming School, I was burning more calories than I was taking in because of the months of intense training. My calorie burn was extreme. It was a very dangerous time for me because when I ate lunch, I didn't have an appetite even though I was cannibalizing my muscle. Muscle cannibalization is when your body breaks down your muscle to get the proper energy and nutrients your body needs to function. It's literally your body eating itself from within; hence the word cannibalization. I knew my body was breaking down and would be just a matter of time before it would quit on me and cause injury.

The next class I was in was a little more challenging than the previous because of body fatigue. This was the time of the swine flu scare, and I was sick as a dog. Now, I'm not saying that I had swine flu, but my friend who lived across the hall had it, and the naval hospital didn't realize it until he was almost over it. In this class, I learned to overcome the most pain I have ever had up to that time. Because of dehydration, my calves would cramp up while we were swimming laps in the water. In Rescue Swimming School, if a student stops swimming due to a muscle cramp, an RSS instructor would jump into the pool and pull the student out. That student would then be rolled out of that class and have to wait a few weeks to join up in the next class. That wasn't an option for me. I knew my body and knew that my body wouldn't be able to continue the intense stress that it had been enduring for the past few months. So I would swim sprints with my class and continue to be one of the top finishers, regardless of the severe pain I felt from cramps in my calves. I learned to overcome that pain, to block it out, once again using thoughts of Jesus and the pain He endured. Jesus had His muscle torn off His bones; what's a muscle cramp compared to that?

Unfortunately, there were some things my mind just couldn't overcome. I decided I had to talk to an instructor about going to the doctor when I noticed blood in my urine. I've never been a person to panic, but when I saw blood where blood wasn't supposed to be, I was sure that I was going to die. But when I went to see the doctor, she told me that I was fine and just needed to be sure that I was drinking plenty of water. She asked me if there was anything else I was concerned about that she could check. As a matter of fact, there was. Sometime during my first class up in RSS, my foot started hurting pretty bad. After awhile, it started feeling a little better, but some kind of bump started growing on top of my foot, right where the fin ran across, which would make training in the water excruciating. Well, when I took my boot off, she showed great concern and sent me to get an X-ray "STAT!" So I went and got an X-ray on my right foot and went back to my room. For some reason, my case fell through the cracks, and I didn't get a call until about three weeks later. After the call, I went back to the doctor to get the results. It turns out that my foot was broken and created bone spurs where the fracture had occurred, thus the great pain when pressure was put on the area, which happened to be the bump where my fin ran across. The doctor then told me that, since so much time had passed, the bone had healed up. All they had to do was open up my foot and scrape the bone spurs out. Up to that moment, I hadn't had many pleasant experiences with Navy medicine, so I refused treatment. Unfortunately, that meant that I would be medically dropped from Rescue Swimming School. (I most likely would have been medically dropped even with the surgery.)

Since I was medically dropped, I was able to choose another job in the Navy. I wanted to stay in the aircrew community because it demanded excellent fitness and great attention to detail. My new job was chosen less for its job description and more for its location to my fiancée. I had just recently gotten engaged to the love of my life, and I knew that location and availability to Susan was top priority. I settled with signing papers to be a "Flight Engineer" on a P-3c Orion. A four turbo prop plane that was too big to land on a ship, which meant it was land based and, more importantly, the training was in Jacksonville, Florida, where my fiancée and I were going to live after we were married.

After graduating Aviation Electronics School in Pensacola and graduating from SERE (Survival Evasion Resistance and Escape) school in San Diego, I was off to Jacksonville to NAS Jax to begin training in Flight Engineer school.

The physical part of F.E. school was laughable, but what it lacked in physical fitness, it made up for in smarts. It was by far the hardest school intellectually that I've ever been a part of. Everything was Japanese to me. In the classroom, I struggled. But, once again, I excelled in the fitness department. After physical training with the F.E. instructors, I would shoot over to the gym and do a high intensity weight lifting session to put on some more pounds and keep in tip-top shape.

Jason and I shortly before the shooting

The great thing about NAS Jax is the command where I was stationed; VP-30. VP-30 was and is like a family. Never have I seen a group of people rally around and support a sailor like VP-30 did when I got injured. I have never been prouder of the Navy and the people that represent and protect the flag because of the family I had at my command.

After all was said and done, I couldn't be prouder of the decision I made to serve my country in the United States Navy. Now, when I look at the flag and hear our national anthem being played, a great emotion wells up inside of me as I remember the oath I took years ago, and I thank the Lord Almighty for the blessing of being born in this great country of ours. I was asked once, if I got to go back in time to the moment I signed on the dotted line, would I do it again. "Yes," I would say. "A hundred times over." Hoo-ya!

CHAPTER 4

SUSAN: THE UNSINKABLE SHIP

A wife of noble character who can find?
She is worth far more than rubies.

~ Proverbs 31:10 NIV

IN THE SUMMER OF MY sophomore year of college, my best friend and I camped out on an island called "Nest Key" located in the Florida Keys. Nest Key is a tiny island filled with mosquitoes, mangroves, and marshes that couldn't be located on any major map. The tiny island got its name because of its being a prime nesting place for the growing bald eagle population in South Florida.

Because of its proximity to the mainland, isolation from humans, and the abundance of food (fish) that surrounds the island, eagles from all over the state of Florida were migrating to this island to breed and nest—hence the name "Nest Key." Unfortunately, the breeding grounds were being compromised due to a rapidly growing population of rats on the island that were swimming from island to island, consuming precious resources and compromising the fragile ecosystem that make up the Florida Keys. I know this, because my mother knows this.

My mother tracks and researches the migrating and behavioral patterns of the American bald eagle in South Florida. She has seen the population grow from year to year because of "safe havens" like Nest Key. But, because of the non-native black rat (radius radius) that recently discovered the island, the past few years have shown a plateau of population growth. This is because the rats go into the eagle's nest and eat the eggs or even the hatchlings while the mother is away looking for food. Although not too serious of a matter at the time, because of the rapid multiplying ability of the rat, the bald eagle population was in grave danger in the near future. This is where Chris and I did our part.

Most of these islands are completely off limits to humans unless

Chris and I

you have a permit. My mother and her husband, Brian, possessed such a permit. Mom hired Chris and me to spend the night on the island and kill as many rats as we could. We were her "Population Control Agents." So on a muggy Saturday afternoon, Mom boated us out to Nest Key in a rinky-dink little raft boat, dropped us off with two tents, some water, a fishing pole, and two BB guns. She wished us luck and told us to expect her back at noon the next day. And since both Chris and I assumed that the other would bring a watch, we had no concept of time. . . except for the sun positioning in the sky, which was the way we liked it. Grabbing our gear, we walked the perimeter of the island to find a decent spot to set up camp for the night. After some time, we found a tiny beach on the south side of the island. The beach was just big enough to pitch both of our tents and have a little room for us to sit around a fire.

Our Nest Key campsite

As the sun was dropping closer to the horizon and the shadows were growing longer on the white sand, I decided to wade out into the water. I walked out until the water was about waist deep. I stood there and looked out into the distance, taking in all the sights and sounds that this location had to offer. For the first time since I could remember, I was completely quiet and repose. The water was clear, warm, and still, and it looked as flat and smooth as glass. It reflected the sky so magnificently that, in the distance, you couldn't tell where the ocean ended and the sky began. The clouds were shades of orange and purple against a blue canvas. The air was warm and sticky with a hint of salt that rested on my tongue with each breath I took. Looking around and seeing all that God had created warmed my heart. For the first time in my life, I saw this beautiful creation and saw what God had created was perfect. God was with me in that moment. It was clear that He was real and was standing right beside me. That experience was so profound to me that I would later state in my "Last Will and Testament" that my ashes were to be sprinkled there. Up until that moment, I'd never seen anything so beautiful, and I thought I never would again. Nine years later, Susan Jeselnik proved me wrong when she opened the door to her sister's house and smiled at me.

Susan Marie Jeselnik was born on November fifth in North Babylon, Long Island, to an Austrian-born father (John) and an

Italian mother (Denise). Susie (as I like to call her) was the youngest of two girls, the eldest being Diane. They lived on Long Island until Susan was about seven years old. That's when they decided to pack their things and move down to Miami, only four miles away from me. Susan was raised training in gymnastics with aspirations of next level competition—and possibly world competition. But, because of a falling out between Susan's mother and her coach, she was pulled out of gymnastics and put into cheerleading. This is where I first came to know who Susan was. Susan was the tumbler on her high school cheerleading team, Miami Palmetto Panthers. A tumbler is a person on the team that does all the back hand springs, flips, and so on. Contrary to popular belief, not all cheerleaders know how to tumble in high school, but because of her history in competitive gymnastics, she was one of the best. You know when you go to a football game and see that girl doing back hand springs from one in-zone to the other and you almost get sick just watching her flip that many times? Well, that was Susie. She would perform back to back to back hand springs and pop up with a huge smile on her face.

Unfortunately, I never had a chance to watch her because while she was on the sidelines cheering, I was on the field playing. Yes, we went to the same high school, but we never dated. I knew who she was by seeing her with the cheerleaders and the fact she dated my best friend briefly. She also attended FCA (Fellowship of Christian Athletes) meetings from time to time, which was held at my house.

Susan has the skin color of her Italian mother and the eyes of her Austrian father, which make a great combination. Her beauty was and still is breathtaking. With her tan skin and her blue/green eyes, all she would have to do is smile and you would be putty in her hands, something I would experience years down the road.

Susan always had an old soul to her. She practiced the morals and temperament of our grandparents. She was a very patient teenager who wasn't all wrapped up in parties and boys like most teenage girls were at that time (from what she tells me). She lived to laugh and loved nothing more than to dance. To know her was to know the sweetest things in life and to forget the dark things that this world has to offer.

After high school, she attended and graduated from Florida State University with a degree in business and moved up to New York to work for Merrill Lynch as a financial consultant for about seven years before transferring back down to Miami. When she moved back down to Miami, I had been long gone for a few years myself. Instead of ending back in Miami, I settled in South Carolina, right down the street from my brother and his wife and kids. You would think that the odds of Susie and I ending up together would be very slim, but, thankfully, it wasn't impossible.

Our generation was just at the foot of the technological mountain. In high school, we had beepers, not cell phones. My freshman year in college was the first time I experienced sending mail electronically. I didn't even call it e-mail. I always referred to it as "sending mail electronically." A few years after, I discovered instant messages and chat rooms. I wasn't fluent in technology, but it wasn't for sake of not trying. Susan, on the other hand, was anti-new technology. She didn't like cell phones or social media sites. She has—and still tells me that she'd be perfectly happy with—a wall-mounted phone with an extended cord and a pen and paper to write letters with. Little did she know that, one day, she would find her husband through social media.

Her family had dinner together on an annual basis. This year, they were traveling to Texas to meet up with the cousins. While Susie was watching TV with her extended family, her cousin, Kristen, offered to set up a Facebook account for Susan so they could keep in touch with each other. Although Susan was opposed to the idea of cluttering her life with hours of status updates and image uploads, she was polite and agreed to be entered into the social media universe.

Around the same time in South Carolina, my sister-in-law, Ginger, basically did the same thing with me, although I wasn't opposed to it; I was just lazy.

A few weeks went by and we did the whole Facebook thing: accept friends, tag, and update our status. Then, one night, while I was hanging out at my brother's house, something happened that changed my life as I knew it.

I logged onto my Facebook account and started accepting friend requests as I'd done for weeks. Most of you know this, but when you accept a friend, this window pops up that states "You Might Have These People In Common," or something like that. Well, that window popped up, and I saw her. There was a picture of Susan with a big smile on her face, hugging her dog, Jessie. Something struck me about that picture. She was beautiful, for sure, but there was something else. I had a feeling that I'd found something I had lost for a long time. It was a sense of relief as well as nervousness.

Feeling nervous similar to how I used to feel right before kickoff in a big game, I pulled up her page and sent her a private message. I said something corny and unassuming like, "Hey you! It's been so long! How are you!?!?" This is when my courtship of her began. I held my cards pretty close to my chest because I didn't want her to think that I was any more interested than just being friendly. But, secretly, I was banging my head against the wall because I liked her so much. Susie was clueless to my motives between our e-mail conversations because the day before I sent her that first private message, I signed a letter of intent to enlist in the United States Navy. She would later tell me that she didn't think I wanted to be tied to a relationship since I was on my way to see the world in the Navy. She was completely unaware that she put the hook in me. I was sold out for her. No other girl, either at the time I met her or future girls I might one day meet, could hold a candle to the woman I was getting to know at that very moment.

Susan leveled me with her mind and her soul. I couldn't believe all the similar interests we shared or the same dislikes. If there ever was a "too good to be true" scenario, this felt like it. I kept waiting for the other shoe to drop, but it never did.

Almost a month went by before we decided to actually see each other in person. She was still in Miami, and I was living in South Carolina. Her sister and husband, Diane and Kenton, were living in Jacksonville, Florida, which was almost exactly halfway between her house and mine. She had mentioned that she would go there to visit from time to time. One night, I said to her that I'd like to take her out for coffee the next time she was in Jacksonville. Up until then, Susan thought I was just being friends with her. Well, I was, but I also wanted to be more than friends. Of course, she accepted, and, yes, I would have driven six hours just to have coffee with her. I liked her that much.

About a week later, she told me that she was going to see her sister and was wondering if I had anything going on that weekend. It didn't matter what I had that weekend, I was going to be free for her. Susan said that driving six hours for a cup of coffee was crazy, and I should just stay in the guest room at her sister's house. I gratefully accepted her invitation and nervously awaited the weekend.

Around nine o'clock Friday night, I pulled into Diane and Kenton's driveway. I managed to squeeze a six and a half hour drive into five hours and fifteen minutes, the whole time fantasizing about the first time I would see her. Leaving my bag in the car for the time being, I walked up to the front door and knocked.

In the beginning of this chapter, I explained that moment on Nest Key and how it was the most beautiful creation I'd ever seen and thought I ever would . . . but Susan blew that moment away.

She opened the door, and my heart left me. It jumped out of my chest and flew straight to her arms. I thought an angel opened the door. Her hair was as dark as the night, and her eyes as bright as the sun. She leveled me with her smile and awakened me with her presence. She was wearing a cream colored sweater

Susan and I

and blue jeans. I knew, right then and there, I was home. I was looking at my future wife, and she was looking right back at me. It was as if time stopped, and we were the only ones in the universe.

A few months later, I asked for Susan's hand in marriage. Not long after, we were married.

Marriage to Susan was one of the best things that has ever happened to me. I truly believe that the Lord chose her for me before I was even conceived here on Earth. And it hadn't been more evident to me until the evening of October 17, 2012:

"Hello?"

"Hello, is this Susan?"

"Yes . . ."

"I just want you to know that your husband's been shot."

"What?"

"Brett has been shot. He's right here. I'm gonna put you on speaker so you can talk to him."

"Okay."

"Baby . . . What's for dinner?"

"Brett? What happened?!?"

"I've been shot. I'm okay though. The ambulance is on the way."

"Okay?"

"Susan, I love you so much."

"I love you! I'm on my way!"

Susan grabbed our son Jason and jumped in the car and drove to where I lay. She saw the ambulance pull out of the parking lot where I had been shot. As the ambulance raced to the hospital, Susie followed close behind. I wouldn't talk to her again for twenty days.

I can't even imagine the hell she went through during those days. The doctors were sure I was going to die. My family began making funeral arrangements, but Susan, with a seventeen-month-old little boy and seven months pregnant with our little girl, was sure that I was going to defy the odds. I was going to look her in the eyes again; I was going to talk to her again. She kept it together the whole time she was in the hospital, talking with the doctors, family, and friends, only to go home and crumble into her mother's arms. She would sob in the shower and fall on her knees, begging the Lord to save her husband. She didn't sleep; she didn't eat. She had to make the choice that no wife should ever have to make: whether or not the doctors should amputate my leg. An urgent decision had to be made over the phone while I was on the operating table. The doctors said that they could save the leg and the infections might go away and I might end up living, or amputate and the infection will go away and the chances of survival could increase dramatically. She told the doctors, "Do whatever you have to do to save my husband's life."

To this day, she asks me if she made the right decision, and time and time again I tell her that other than marrying me, this was the best decision she's ever made. I tell her that she saved my life, and I thank her often for her courage.

She believes in loyalty, love, and unending patience. Without all three of these qualities, she wouldn't have survived. My injuries would have been too hard. Too much work. But the Lord knew what He was doing when He brought Susan into my life. He saw this day before He made me out of dirt. And He knew that I would need a woman of faith, of hope, and of love. Susan Parks has all these, and I thank the Lord for her every day. She is the glue that holds our family together. She is the sun on a rain drenched afternoon. She is my heart, and I will forever be grateful for each and every breath that I take by her side. I love you, Susan.

CHAPTER 5

FROM TRAINING TO TEACHING: BECOMING A CERTIFIED TRAINER

Do you not know that your body is a temple of the Holy Spirit
within you, whom you have from God? You are not your own, for you
were bought with a price. So glorify God in your body.

~ 1 Corinthians 6:19–20 ESV

FROM A VERY EARLY AGE, fitness was a part of my everyday life. I grew up in the era when your parents kicked you out of the house to play until dinner time. Once you heard Mom's whistle, no matter where you were or what you were doing, you made a bee line straight home as fast as you could.

Being outside all the time meant doing outside things. My brother and I would ride our bikes six miles to the nearest Wendy's restaurant for a "Frosty" and ride our bikes back. On a daily basis, especially in the summer time, journeys like "The Wendy's Expedition" would occur.

We would find fresh piles of tree trimmings and pile them up to a dump pile fort. Those were always fun times. Even though picking up those heavy branches and pulling them next to the street would tire us out, it was always worth it in the end. We felt like we were Ewoks from Star Wars and we were building our tree forts, waiting for the Empire to show up.

Everything I did as a child was active. I wasn't like many kids today who sit on their couches and play Xbox games or chat on their computer for hours. I waited until I became an adult. Don't get me wrong, I had Atari and later Nintendo, but the time that I could play was strictly enforced. A half hour on the weekend was the longest I could play, and it usually ended with my brother and me getting into a fight because one of us beat the other in Techno Bowl. Then, outside we went.

When I started getting older, I went from running and bike riding to playing football. I always had a football in my arms, and whenever my friends and I gathered, we played football. Sometimes I had to play basketball, but football was the game of choice for me. That kept me quick on my feet and toughened me up, especially when I played with my brother's friends who were three years older than I. I always enjoyed playing with them because they never took me seriously due to my age and size. But once somebody gave me a shot and threw me the ball, they rarely kept me from scoring.

Once I learned about lifting weights, I was enthralled. The combination of all the physical activity I would do outside and the lifting of weights inside changed my life. I could see my body going from a lean runner's body to a bulkier decathlete's body. My muscles were starting to grow. I felt stronger than I had ever felt before. Not only that, but I was feeling all around better. I was always a very lean person, weighing an average of 165 pounds, so I wanted to see if I could get my body to 190 pounds. I set a goal, wrote a workout and eating program for myself, and went at it. In six months, I reached my goal. I gained twenty-five pounds of lean muscle and had only six percent body fat, which is pretty darn good.

I loved seeing how my body changed by lifting weights and eating right. But I wanted to know and understand more of why certain foods are good and certain lifts combined with each other are the most effective. So I started looking around for an online CPT (Certified Personal Trainer) course. An online course worked really well for me because I could work around my busy work schedule and also go at my own pace.

The CPT course I chose was from NESTA (National Exercise Science Trainers Association). NESTA really concentrated on the kinesiology and anatomy of an exercise as well as proper form and technique. When I first got involved in becoming a certified personal trainer, it was just so I could learn more for my health and wellness. It wasn't until after I became certified that I realized how many people would actually pay me to train them. So being a teacher in the weight room was my new side job.

I loved training a person in the gym. There is no greater feeling than seeing a kid go from being unable to lift the barbell (forty-five lbs.) to being able to lift the barbell plus thirty pounds on it (seventy-five lbs.) only three weeks later. He has a look of a conqueror, as if he just defeated the world and was standing on top of it. It was such a great feeling, when a person puts their trust in you, and you come through for them. When they see results, it's very satisfying. But, sometimes we worked out for weeks without seeing results, without a change in my client's body fat percentage drop or strength increase. I got a lot of flak from those clients and, before we would go any further, I would ask them about their diet. They would describe an awful eating regiment the majority of the time. I would stop them right there and tell them the reason they don't see results is because of what they are putting in their body. I would explain their diet is eighty percent of the equation and working out with me is just twenty percent. I could look after them only twenty percent of the time. The other eighty percent was completely on them. I was never afraid of losing a client. I knew that if they trusted me and listened to what I said regarding diet and weight lifting, they would see positive results. It takes hard work and commitment, and if you were "firing" me, it was probably more because of you rather than me. Does that sound arrogant? I don't mean it to be. It's like that with most fitness trainers.

I was even giving speed and conditioning lessons at a few neighborhood parks. Depending on what sport my client wanted to excel in, I had certain drills for speed, quickness, and agility. Some of my clients just wanted to be bigger, faster, and stronger all around, so I started up boot camp sessions. My boot camp sessions weren't like the traditional ones you might see on the beach or in the park on a Saturday morning; I trained with a completely different philosophy. I believe that you can reach the same—if not better—results by doing heart rate elevating and sustaining exercising without ever having to run. I know how much people hate running and how boring it can be. So, being in Rescue Swimming School and Aircrew School in the Navy gave me a lot of ideas. I integrated a lot of the land based workouts as well as some "H.I.T." (High Intensity Training) lifts. Not only are you burning fat in my boot camp classes, but you're also building muscle. And this was a result that my clients loved. They continually kept coming back for more.

Being a certified fitness trainer is a twenty-four hour, seven days a week job. If you're not designing someone's workout routine or training a client, you're at home, studying and getting your "continuing education credits." Most legit CFT certifications have continuing education credits in order to maintain your certifications. Just like in the medical field, the fitness field is always changing. A certified fitness trainer needs to be savvy on the latest discoveries about the human body and its response to certain exercises. As I write this, I'm in the process of learning about "Strength Training for the Combat Athlete." The best kind of fitness trainer is the one who constantly tries to better himself, both in and out of the gym.

Physical appearance is very important as well for a certified fitness trainer. You wouldn't want to go to a doctor with a dirty lab coat or a dietitian who's obese, so of course you wouldn't want to be trained by a fitness trainer who looks like he has never lifted a weight before. Since the first time I worked out with my dad in our garage my freshman year in high school, I've been hooked on weights. I've always been motivated to run, lift weights, swim, and any other technique to stay fit. So I have always had an appearance of being fit. So, when I give advice about a certain lift or how to develop a certain muscle, I have a little more clout due to the fact that I've been in the weight room for over fifteen years.

Appearance isn't everything though. You see a lot of these gargantuan men in some of these gyms. Many think that at the size they are, they are qualified to instruct others in strength conditioning. In many cases, it isn't true. These men, called "Meat Heads," are usually on some kind of growth hormone. They know what lifts work for them but don't necessarily know what will work for others. Everybody is different. And this is where the certification comes in. Ideally, if you find a person who is fit and educated, you've got a qualified trainer. This is the kind of trainer that I've tried to be, a trainer who is continuously trying to better himself both in mind and body. Even with my setbacks, I won't stay out of the gym. Although I'm not working out as hard as I used to (right now), I still won't throw in the towel. My fitness level was one of the reasons I survived all the surgeries after I was shot. During the first twenty days after the incident, I had over a dozen surgeries. Without the Lord instilling fitness in me at such a young age and keeping me motivated to work as hard as I did, I wouldn't have survived. So I owe it to the weight room to keep pushing. And keep pushing, I will.

CHAPTER 6

DON'T FORGET THE MILK: TAKING MY LIFE FOR GRANTED

"How quickly we forget God's great deliverances in our lives. How easily we take for granted the miracles he performed in our past."

~ David Wilkerson

SO MANY THINGS RUN THROUGH your head when you're lying face down in a condominium complex expecting to die. Other than the searing pain that's shooting through your body (no pun intended), you think about everything. Not only do you think about your past, but you also think about your future.

The very first thing that I said to myself was "You gotta be kidding me!" I couldn't believe I got shot. I kept thinking this seemed to be some movie plot that was playing out. I was living a perfect life with a perfect family, but then a gunman tried to take it all away from me without a hesitation. "What a good movie this will make." It's a strange first thought, but who looks for reason in a dying man anyway?

The first person I thought of was my wife. I thought about how she was going to handle being a widow with a seventeen-month-old boy and two more months of pregnancy to go with our baby girl. Lying there, I missed her so much. All I wanted was to feel her warm body against mine and kiss her lips one more time. I knew that I would never see her smile again on this side of heaven.

I thought about my son. That little boy thought the world of me. Everywhere I went, he tagged along, yes, even to the restroom. Because of him, everything I did became a team sport. From showering to using the bathroom, nothing was off limits to him. I wondered what kind of a man he was going to be. Will he be bitter growing up without his father? Will he love the Lord with all his heart? Will he be a man of character and integrity?

I thought about Stella. She was my beautiful little girl that was two months away from being born into this world. I'd never get to look in her eyes. Never get to see her smile. Crawl. Walk. I'd never get to meet the boys she will someday bring home. Never get to sit them down and ask them uncomfortable questions while cleaning my gun. I'd never get to see her graduate. Never walk her down the aisle. But, most importantly, I'd never get to see her.

Believe it or not, all of these things went through my head. It probably took about a second to think of all these things, but it felt like an eternity.

It was nothing short of a miracle I survived. But it made me look back at my life and assess what kind of life I lived. I grew up in the church, and I gave my life to Jesus when I was about eight years old. But I never really tried to live more like Jesus.

As Christians, we are called to live like Jesus. In the world we live in today, it could be a difficult thing to do if you are only half committed to Jesus and the ministry He has called upon us to spread. Don't get me wrong, Jesus was doing works in me since I asked Him into my heart, but I resisted much of the time. Of course I would have my periods where I was "on fire" for God and would be full throttle, but this feeling would eventually wear off, and I'd be back doing the same old, same old with people that were no good for me.

When I was twenty-nine years old, I ran into an old acquaintance who ended up becoming my wife. God was in the details there, and I was very grateful. The Lord has always been with me, refining me. He has been molding me from the beginning. But I was too busy doing other things to realize it. The Lord blessed me with a wonderful family, a beautiful wife, a healthy son, and a daughter on the way but I was too busy complaining and being ungrateful to realize everything I had.

The Lord calls Christians to be obedient to Him, but I wasn't. I heard Him calling to me, but I had something else going on. Then, October 17th happened.

I remember two days before, talking to my client about when she would like her first session to be. We agreed on Wednesday at 6:30 in front of her fitness center. I remember Susan asked me to get milk that day and had given me a coupon for it. So, Wednesday, I kissed my son goodbye and kissed Susan, told her that I loved her and walked out the door. About five minutes later, I ran back in to the house to grab the coupon from the kitchen table. I quickly gave Susan another kiss and yelled that I loved her as I ran out the door. If I had known this may have been our last kiss or the last "I love you," I would have savored it a little more or maybe even have taken my time and really said a true goodbye, but, no, I was in a hurry.

This seemed like my life up until 6:30 that evening. Everything was rushed. I was always in a hurry. Never stopped and really savored much at all. I was a good husband before the incident and a good father, but I could have been better. My Christian life was good, but it could have been better. Way better.

Had I died that fateful night, what kind of legacy would I have left behind? When I got to heaven, would Jesus say, "Well done, my son," or would He say, "What happened? I gave you so many opportunities and you squandered them"? That scared me. Even to this day.

In the Bible, Jesus says that many will say to Him, "Lord, Lord, did we not prophesy in your name and in your name drive out demons and in your name perform many miracles?" Then Jesus would say to them, "I never knew you. Away from me, you evildoers!" (Matthew 7:22–23).

That passage affected me because even though these men were evil doers and didn't know the Lord, they were out doing something! I was more of a sideline Christian. I loved the Lord, but I wasn't out telling people about Him. I knew that there was a God and that He sent His Son to die on the cross for my sins, but my God seemed very distant. He was way up there, and we were all the way down here. The Lord and I had a relationship, but it felt very one sided most of the time.

What kind of person had I become? When did I start feeling so entitled to everything? What kind of person thinks God is there for them and not the other way around? Well, the truth is, many of us have become this person in one way or another at one time in our lives. I believe, especially in America, we don't serve enough for the Lord. Words like serve, surrender, or obedience are viewed as negative terms. The tragedy is those are key words in Christian ministry. Many times I felt the Lord prodding me in a certain direction, but I went another way because it didn't fit in my worthless schedule.

After the incident, in the hospital, through tears of thankfulness, I told the Lord I would go wherever He led me. I told Him I surrendered and asked Him to help me be obedient.

Now, don't get me wrong; there are still times I want to go with my own agenda, but this is what makes us human. I just continue with my prayer to the One Most High: "Lord, I just want to be obedient to you. Help me to be obedient."

CHAPTER 7

THE FEAR

So do not fear, for I am with you; do not be dismayed, for I am
your God. I will strengthen you and help you; I will uphold you with
my righteous right hand.

~ Isaiah 41:10 NIV

AUGUST OF 1991, I WAS living in South Florida in an old house in Miami. I was thirteen years old and enjoying the last few weeks of summer before starting my 8th grade year in middle school. A tropical wave in the middle of the Atlantic Ocean didn't seem like a big deal to us hardened storm warriors. Storms like these would spring up from the tropics all the time. We would just get out our skim boards and trek out into the storm to surf the cold puddles and slide head first onto the saturated grass. When this tropical wave grew into a hurricane, we laughed. When it became a category 5 hurricane, we worried. The name Andrew will forever be synonymous with the hurricane that made landfall on August 24, 1991, and changed our lives forever.

I remember my brother and I were so excited that night. We loved big storms, especially hurricanes. Something about the wind and lightning really amazed us. It was tough for us to fall asleep that night because we didn't want to miss the storm. We didn't have to worry about that because a few hours later, we were awakened by the ceiling collapsing on us. I remember the fear I felt. Never before have I feared for my life. I was sure that Hurricane Andrew was going to sweep me up and pull me out into the dark waters in the ocean, forever separating me from my family.

The wind gusts got up to 250 miles per hour. It sounded as if there were a speeding locomotive right outside our house. The wind was so strong, it ripped all the plywood off all the windows in the first fifteen minutes of the storm (it had taken my dad, brother, and me about eight hours to put plywood over all the windows). My family and I had to rush into our cramped laundry room before the winds sucked us out. Before we made it, one of our sliding glass doors shattered in on my brother and cut him up pretty bad.

So here we were, bloodied, wet, and scared. I remember sitting by the laundry room door and watching the wooden door bowing in and out as the wind blew against the outer panel. I told my dad the door looked like it was about to blow in on us. After a quick inspection, my dad and brother began holding the laundry room door closed as the wind was trying to blow it open. That speeding locomotive was now in my kitchen, pounding on the laundry room door, demanding to be let in.

As if battling the winds weren't enough, the flood waters began to rush in the room right under my dad and brother's feet.

I grabbed a bucket as quickly as I could and started bailing the water into our deep sink. It was a tiresome effort and felt hopeless. The water rushed in faster than I could bail, but I couldn't just throw my hands up in the air and surrender to the storm.

For over four hours, my dad and brother held that door shut, and I bailed the flood waters. We survived Andrew, but we were scared for our lives. I've never felt fear like that before and haven't since—that is, not until October 17th, 2012.

It's a strange emotion, fear. People react to fear in different ways. Some become paralyzed, some run, and some may even attack what they fear. But, one thing's for sure; we all have experienced fear in one way or another.

Wednesday, October 17, 2012, I was on my way out the door for a 6:30 personal training session. My client and I agreed a few days before what day and time worked best for her. Susan had a coupon for a gallon of milk for my son and asked that I go by the store and pick it up for her after the training session. I gave Susan and Jason (who was seventeen months old at the time) a kiss and told Susie that I loved her. I've always made a point never to leave the house without telling my wife that I love her.

The ride to my client's fitness center is about a twenty-minute drive, so I took that time to make some finishing tweaks and touches on the session. I'd never been to the housing complex where my client's fitness center was located, so I parked by the front office where I assumed the fitness center was. I took all my stuff out of my car, which included a step up platform, two speed ladders, and some cones, and placed them in front of the fitness building. I was a few minutes early, so I wasn't expecting her right away, which was a good thing; I tend to get nervous meeting people that I'm training for the first time. Maybe it's just the fear of not producing for them. But I was relieved that I still had a few extra minutes to spare.

While standing there outside the fitness center, I saw a young man walking up from the parking lot. He wore baggy jeans that sagged below his waist and a green hooded sweat shirt with pockets in the front. He looked out of place, and I immediately had an unsettling feeling about him. I remember being upset at myself for being so stereotypical and thinking this guy probably lives here and is just coming home from work. I decided to make up for my poor judgment and acknowledged him with a "what's up" and a head nod. "Sup," came the reply as he gave an equal head nod. We briefly made eye contact and then went about our business: me, standing and waiting; he, walking toward and then behind the fitness center. I was still uneasy about him, especially after the eye contact. There was something cold about his eyes; like the eyes of a shark, they were emotionless, unwavering.

While waiting, a lady came walking by with her dogs. I smiled as she approached, and I bent over to pet the dogs. We had a brief conversation about them as I told her about my little dog. Then she continued on her way, walking toward a patch of grass, and once again, I continued to stand there and wait for my client, who was now late.

It seemed only about a minute went by when I heard a noise I've never wanted to hear in my life and still haunts me to this day. I heard a scream. This wasn't any kind of scream. It was a scream from a grown man. It was a kind of scream that makes the hair on the back of your neck stand up and makes your heart start pumping so hard that it seems people can hear it thumping from miles away.

On full alert, I began cautiously walking in the direction of the scream, which came from behind the fitness center. The lady with the dogs had a full view of the building and yelled out in a panic, "Oh my gosh! He's being robbed! Somebody help him!"

I didn't hear the last part too well because the second I heard "robbed," I started sprinting toward the place I heard the scream. As I turned the corner, I saw a young man spin his head around at me. I made eye contact with the same cold eyes that I felt so unsure about just minutes before. My instincts had been right. This was a bad man. When he saw me, he jumped the pool gate to try and get back to his getaway car, that—unbeknownst to me at the time—had three or four of his buddies in it. Who knows what would have happened if I hadn't run up at that moment? The victim yelled out, "He just robbed me! He just robbed me!" I had a choice to make. I could either turn and walk away, or I could try and stop the robber. No matter what decision I made, I had involved myself, and my life was going to be changed forever.

I remembered the promise that I made to the Lord back in high school about never walking by a person in need again. If I walk away, I break my promise to God, but if I help, I fulfill my oath. I had a huge problem that was overcoming me as the seconds ticked by. I was scared, and the closer I came to my decision, the more fearful I became . . . because I knew the choice I was going to make.

I hear people talk about courage all the time, and I think it may be misused in many situations. I know that by definition, courage is the ability to do something that you know is right or good, even though it is dangerous, frightening, or very difficult. This man had to be stopped, at least until the police arrived and could hash the situation out. So I turned and ran around the fitness center to try and cut him off. "Call the police!" I said to the lady walking her dogs as I ran by. I was pretty sure there was only one way out of this housing complex and, as long as I stood between him and the road out, he was trapped until the police arrived.

The last thing I wanted was to get into a confrontation. But an injustice was done, and I wasn't going to let this guy just get away with it. My heart was pounding, my adrenaline was pumping, and I had fear coursing through my veins.

The perpetrator ran through the condo complex, and I was about to chase after him when the victim yelled to me that his getaway car was right behind me. Sure enough, right behind where I stood, parked with the engine running, was his car and four of his buddies. I turned around and quickly took my phone from my pocket. I figured that if I didn't catch the guy, I would have a picture of his license plate. Being very new to a smart phone and my adrenaline pumping so hard that my hands wouldn't stop shaking, I couldn't get a picture, at least, not a clear one. This was when I saw him again.

The young man with the cold eyes decided to backtrack and try and escape by going back through the pool area and behind the fitness center; pretty smart, if you ask me. I saw him just as he stepped into the parking lot, trying to run with his saggy pants. Needless to say, I ran him down pretty quickly.

I grabbed him by his shoulders and proceeded to walk with him, both of us doing a brisk side shuffle.

"Where you goin'?" I said.

"Let me go, dawg," he said.

I noticed that he had his hands in his sweatshirt pocket, which seemed kind of odd to me. "You're not going anywhere. The cops are on their way. You're done." I said, expecting him to raise one of his arms to take a swing at me.

"Let me go, dawg," he said another time.

"Nope. You're done," I said to him.

Then, I heard two shots that brought back the deepest kind of fear that has been absent from my life ever since Hurricane Andrew. I'd been shot. This was it. This is my last day on Earth.

CHAPTER 8

THE SHOT HEARD AROUND MY WORLD

Finally, be strong in the Lord and in the strength of his might.

~ Ephesians 6:10 ESV

WHEN I WAS GROWING UP, I always watched violent movies. I loved action movies. I loved a guy who would jump out of a helicopter and into a speeding car and, at the same time, be getting shot at and defusing a nuclear bomb. I really ate stuff like that up. A building would explode into a million pieces, and our main character (usually Arnold Schwarzenegger) would walk out of the rubble with only a little blood trickling from his head. I thought that, like in the movies, when a person was shot, it was no big deal. You get shot, you grunt, and you keep going. Well, reality kicked in the moment I heard those two shots. Less than a foot away from the gun, I was hit, and unlike the movies, I fell like a load of bricks.

I hit the concrete face down. There was a searing pain in my stomach, and I felt a burning tingle throughout my right leg. I've been shot. I was sure that I was shot twice: once in the stomach and once in the leg. I lifted my head and looked at my leg and noticed that it was positioned in a weird way. I thought at the time that the bullet broke a bone, causing it to be turned in that way.

In both pain and panic, I yelled for someone to help me. I heard the gunman run away from the scene. I tried to get up but couldn't move much more than my head and arms. I then laid my head on the warm parking lot pavement and started thinking.

One of the thoughts that entered my mind was *I'm going to die today. This is my last day on Earth. I am so upset. I can't believe that I'm going to die this way.*

My son. My son's not going to have a father. What kind of man is he going to grow up to be? What kind of legacy have I left him?

My daughter. I'll never get to see my daughter. I'll never get to look into her eyes and tell her how much I love her. I'll never get to walk her down the aisle. I wonder what she'll look like. What kind of man will she marry?

My wife. My beautiful wife. I made a promise to her. I promised a long life together. I'm going to break that promise. She's seven months pregnant. I hope she'll be okay. I wish she was here. I want to hold her one more time. I want to feel her body against mine, feel her heart beating. I want to kiss her lips one more time, look into her eyes. How long will it be before I see her again in heaven? Will she want to see me, or would she have found someone else—someone better? I can't believe I'm going to die this way. I'm so upset.

All these thoughts raced through my head in an instant, even though it felt like eternity. I didn't scream it. I didn't even yell or say it. But in a whisper, I said, "Lord, I'm coming to see you today."

I tried again to get up or at least to move, when a man came running up to me and crashed down by my side. "Don't move! I'm a nurse! Don't move! Stay perfectly still!"

I was relieved that someone was there, talking to me. I told him my name, rank, and serial code. I guess my military training kicked in.

After talking with him for a brief moment, I laid my head down on the ground and prepared to die. Once again, in a whisper, I said, "Lord, help me. I need you now. Please, help me." Then, something prompted me to look up. The sun was setting and the sky was beautiful. There was something familiar to the purple and orange clouds against the blue sky. I've seen this before. I've felt this before. Nest Key! It was when I was on Nest Key! God was with me, I felt Him right next to me then. God is with me now.

I felt peace. It was a peace that washed over me, telling me that everything was going to be fine. At that moment, I looked to my left, and there I saw a young woman with dark hair and fair skin. She was on her knees about five feet away from me. With her hand extended out toward me and her head bowed, she was praying in a way that I couldn't understand. As soon as I looked her way, she stopped praying and looked up at me. We made eye contact. I wanted to give her a thumb's up or extend my hand to her so I could pray with her, but I didn't have the strength to move, so I just nodded my head in approval. I wanted her to know I was happy that she was praying, and I didn't want her to stop. As soon as I nodded my head, she bowed hers and started praying again. Then, I laid my head back down. My mentality changed in an instant. I went from "I'm going to die today" to "I'm going to live."

Later, when the police started interviewing the witnesses on the scene, three out of the six people on the scene claimed to have seen the woman. The other three said she wasn't there. The police searched for her with no success. She wasn't a resident of the housing complex or working in the surrounding area. The groundskeeper of the complex said that he turned around as soon as he heard the gunshots, and she was already there, on her knees, praying. He also added that he worked there every day and had never seen her before. I made direct eye contact with her and she was only five feet away from me, but I can't remember what she looks like. The only thing that comes to mind is dark hair and fair skin. Draw your own conclusions, but I'm convinced that she was my angel, praying on my behalf. I hope I get to see her again. She's going to get a big hug.

At the gym, before you design your workout plan, you need to set a goal. There are two kinds of goals that you set: a macro goal and a micro goal. To explain it the easiest, your macro goal would be to be able to squat 400 pounds in six months. But your micro goal would be the weight that you wanted to lift this week. For example, I'm going to squat 225 pounds three times on my fifth set every day. There were also two goals that I set the evening I was shot. My macro goal was that I was going to live. My micro goal was that I was going to stay awake until I arrived at the hospital. I needed to stay awake because I knew if I were to fall asleep, I'd never wake up again—at least, not on this side of heaven. I couldn't reach my macro goal unless I fulfilled my micro goal. It turned out that staying awake was going to be more challenging than I thought.

A crowd had gathered in the parking lot. The lady with the dogs was close enough that I could talk to her. I asked her if she could do me a favor. She agreed, and I proceeded to ask her to get my phone out of my left front pocket and call my wife. I told her that it was under the name "ICE" (In Case of Emergency).

I heard her say into the phone, "Hi. Is this Brett's wife? Your husband's been shot. He's right here. He wants to talk to you. I'm gonna put you on speaker and hold you up to him, okay? Hold on." Now, I'm a guy who never wants my wife to stress about anything. I never want her to know that something's a big deal or I'm hurting or in trouble in any way. I don't like to see her upset if there's nothing she can do about it. I knew her knowing that I'd been shot was freaking her out enough. I knew if my voice shook or I expressed any kind of pain or fear, it could send her into hysterics, so I said the first thing I could think of: "Hey, baby, what's for dinner?"

I heard a nervous chuckle on the other end of the line. She asked what happened, and I told her I'd been shot, that it was no big deal and the ambulance was on its way. I told her I'd see her a little later and said to her the words I thought I might say to her for the last time:

"I love you so much. So much."

At that moment, the lady with the dogs gave the phone to someone I didn't recognize. He ended up staying on the phone with my wife until the ambulance started back to the hospital with me in it.

It seemed like a day and a half before the ambulance arrived. Every second that went by, my energy and strength were draining away. With each blink, my eyelids were getting heavier and heavier. First, the police showed up and asked me what happened. I told the officer I had gone to the aid of a guy being robbed, and I got shot twice: once in the stomach and once in the leg. Then, I proceeded with my name, rank, and serial code. The police officer wanted to keep me awake, so he started asking me questions. That's when I told him that I had a wife, a son, and a little girl on the way. The officer held my hand and asked me more questions. At one point, I couldn't answer him. I was staring straight up to the sky and couldn't move. That was as close to dying at the scene of a crime that I ever got.

I remember realizing I was dying and trying to snap out of it and come back to consciousness. The officer kept telling me to answer him and to hold on, just keep holding on. The police officer later told the press he never felt a person's hand go cold in his until that night. I finally revived and told him I was okay.

After some time, the fire rescue showed up, and we did the same song and dance again. This time, my words were slower, and my eyes were dimmer. Then the paramedics showed up. They asked me where I was shot. I told them the stomach and leg, and they proceeded to turn me over. This made me feel so much better because I had been on my stomach for so long.

The pain was agonizing as the darkness overtook dusk and a big crowd gathered to see the carnage. The paramedic, looking for my gunshot wounds, cut off all my clothes, leaving me butt naked in front of all the spectators. I remember feeling very insecure at the time and, while being inspected by the paramedic, took my hands and covered my man parts. The paramedic couldn't believe it and kind of laughed and said, "Don't worry, Brett. Nobody's looking at that."

I said, "Yeah, right!" So the other paramedic got a little towel and covered the area for me. I was very grateful. I was also surprised when the paramedic said that I'd only been shot once, in the abdomen. I didn't understand why my leg was numb and hurting so much. I thought that maybe I just landed wrong when I fell. I had no idea at the time that the bullet traveled down and completely severed my inferior vena cava, which is the largest vein in the body, the vein that carries the blood to the heart.

I was told later that I was shot in what the military medicine manuals call the "surgical soul" of the body. The combat medic who told me this said if a person gets shot in this particular area, there's no hope; they're as good as dead. I also didn't know at the time that the bullet shredded my right kidney and also blew up a third of my colon. This was serious. I was dying. My denial, stubbornness, and reliance on my Creator were what kept me going. If I had known how serious my condition was at the time, I might have panicked and bled out right there in the parking lot.

I was put into the ambulance, and we made our way to the hospital. In tremendous pain, I asked the paramedic if it was bad. He said that it wasn't bad at all, and I should be fine. I wanted to believe him, but I saw some doubt in his eyes. I knew it was more than he let on because he kept asking me questions to keep me awake. I was staring off into the distance, about to fall asleep, but he wouldn't let me. And I refused to give up. I had a goal to reach, and I was going to reach it. (I met him a year or so later and asked him why he said it wasn't that bad [while laughing]. He responded by saying, "We're not in the habit of telling critically wounded patients the truth.")

By the time we got to the hospital, I was spent. I reached my goal, but I wasn't done yet. I wanted the doctors to put me to sleep. I wanted them to put me under. I wanted it to be controlled. By this time, my eyes were rolling in the back of my head. I could still hear everything, and I was still alert, but I couldn't really keep my eyes open anymore. I heard all the doctors talking back and forth. Talking about my one gunshot wound and there being no exit wound and all kinds of doctor lingo that I didn't understand at the time. What caught my attention big time was hearing a doctor say to his colleague, "We need to intubate him."

To those who don't know, intubation is when the doctors stick a tube all the way down your throat/wind pipe to allow proper airway. I've seen this before and felt queasy every time I saw an individual with one. And I didn't want to be awake when they intubated me. So, with my eyes closed, I asked the doctor, "Are you gonna put me under first?"

I heard a little laugh, and the doctor replied, "Yes, Mr. Parks, we're gonna put you under."

After some orders were barked between the doctors, the last thing I remember was one of the nurses coming up beside me and asking me how I felt. My voice sounded weak and distant. "I'm hurting . . . I'm scared . . ."

I obtained my goal. But my fight for survival had just begun. Every day for the next twenty days, I was written off as dead. Only a miracle could save me. But I had a secret the surgeons didn't know about. I believe in a God that made me out of dust and wasn't about to let me die until He said I could. And He is made perfect in my weakness, as we will see in the coming days.

CHAPTER 9

WHEN I AM WEAK, HE IS STRONG

Fear not, for I am with you; be not dismayed, for I am your God;
I will strengthen you, I will help you, I will uphold you with my righ-
teous hand.

~ Isaiah 41:10 ESV

WHEN MY SON, JASON, WAS two years old (after the incident), he started to be very independent. He didn't need any help when it came to playing and exploring the yard. He would say to me, "Daddy, outside?" I would open the door to the back porch, and off he would go. Running around the yard and talking aloud to whoever may be listening. Every day that passed, he became more confident in his abilities.

My wife and I always made a point to do things together as a family. From making a quick run to the drug store to going grocery shopping, Susan, Stella, Jason, and I would all be packed in the car together. When we went grocery shopping, Jason never wanted to be in the cart. He always wanted to be the guy pushing the cart. He didn't realize how heavy the cart was, especially when it was full of groceries. As confident in his strength as he was, when it was time to push the cart down the aisle, he couldn't budge it. Try as he may, it wouldn't move an inch. He would push with all his might, even to the point of getting a grunt out. Then, after all his efforts, it would begin to move. He had a determined look on his face as the cart moved at a more rapid pace, following mommy. When mommy turned the corner and started walking down the next aisle, Jason would maneuver the cart and make a long "U-Turn" to the next aisle. He was perfect, stopping when he had to stop, avoiding other shoppers and their carts. He even backed the cart up when Mommy passed an item she needed.

Jason felt accomplished. He felt confident. He felt like he was a part of the shopping experience. But what Jason didn't realize was his daddy was right over him, pushing the shopping cart for him. Jason was too weak to push the cart on his own, let alone turn it to avoid other shoppers. So I was there, pushing, stopping, maneuvering, turning, and backing up. Jason may have known I was helping, but I doubt it. He could not have accomplished what he had without me there aiding him. When he was too weak, I was strong.

This was my experience in the hospital the first four months of my recovery, but more so the first twenty plus days after the shooting. The night I was shot, I was training for an eight-mile obstacle course and had slimmed down from 205 pounds to 191 pounds and was probably in the best shape of my life. I was bench pressing 315 pounds and dead lifting 325 pounds on a bad day. I was doing twenty pull ups and burpees like it was nobody's business. I was, for all intents and purposes, a beast. Then I got shot. Even though I had all this strength and all this stamina, I was weak. This was something I couldn't train for. I couldn't strengthen my organs or my arteries. I couldn't be strong enough so that a bullet would bounce off me. I wasn't Superman (although that would have been cool).

Once I got to the hospital at U.F. Health, they put me under. I was in a medically induced coma for twenty days, and I didn't really come to my senses until about five days after that. During that time, I underwent fourteen surgeries. Fourteen surgeries in twenty days is quite a feat. When I got to the hospital, the doctors found that there was a hematoma where the bullet entered. A hematoma is a blood bubble (if you will) that pools the blood and doesn't allow it to escape. Without the hematoma in my body, I would have bled out at the scene. Some may call that luck or coincidence; I call it the hand of God holding the blood in my body so I wouldn't die. The stats show that, where my gunshot wound was located (called the surgical soul), ninety-nine percent of victims bleed out at the scene.

He is strong.

A hematoma is very fragile. One little bump in the road and a hematoma would burst, allowing the blood to flow out of my body. The hospital was a good twenty minutes away, with many bumps and pot holes in the road. I vividly remember hitting what felt like a pot hole the size of a moon crater a few times. Once again, stats of the one percent who make it into the ambulance, ninety-nine percent of them die on the way to the hospital. It's important to note that the ambulance passed a few hospitals on the way to U.F. Health. This was because U.F. Health has the only trauma center in the city of Jacksonville, aptly named "Trauma One." If the paramedics had stopped at any of the hospitals on the way to U.F. Health, my chance of survival would have quite possibly gone from very slim to none.

He is strong.

Once I made it to the hospital and they put me under with all the doctors ready to work on me, God took His hand off my hematoma, and the blood went everywhere. At one point, I had six hands in my stomach trying to stop the bleeding. The doctors later told me that they had my blood all the way up to their elbows and all over their scrubs. Of the one percent of victims that survive the ambulance ride, ninety-nine percent of them bleed out in the emergency room. But our God is a powerful God and put the right doctors in the right places at the right time.

He is strong.

Because I was losing so much blood, I had to have constant blood transfusions. Transfusion after transfusion. They couldn't get enough blood in me because more was bleeding out than they could put back in. In total, the first few days, I had fifty-one units of blood transfused in me and lost thirteen liters of blood. To put it in perspective, go ahead and put six, two-liter soda bottles on the table. I lost more than what you see. I depleted the blood bank. I was supposed to die. The doctors gave me six hours to live. They told my wife to start making funeral arrangements. But after six hours passed, I was still alive. Six hours turned to eight, then twelve. The doctors were baffled.

He is strong.

When the doctors opened me up, they saw the damage that the 9mm bullet did to my insides. My kidney had been shredded beyond recognition. One of the surgeons said my kidney looked like someone put it in a blender and shredded it on high. Because of this trauma and the shock my body had gone through, my other kidney had shut down completely. I would be on dialysis for the next two months.

They also saw my colon. A third of my colon had exploded like somebody put a firecracker in it. Questions arose if I would be "regular" ever again, if, of course, I survived this whole ordeal, which was becoming less than likely in the doctors eyes as they discovered new issues through the wreckage. Because of my colon removal, I would have to have an ileostomy bag for the next six months.

They also saw what the bullet did to my inferior vena cava. The bullet went directly through the artery. The surgeon said that there was a nice round bullet hole straight through. The doctors had to cut and tie off the right

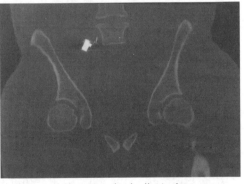

CT scan showing the bullet's damage

femoral then perform a fem to fem bypass to get blood flowing back into my leg. The surgery was a success and the doctors could feel a pulse in my right foot once again. It was a weak pulse, but a pulse nonetheless. One of the fourteen surgeries during this time consisted of a double fasciotomy. This is when the surgeons cut the skin and let the muscle hang out to help relieve the area with swelling. My double fasciotomy was on my right leg on either side of my calf. My leg looked pretty nasty, but there was a pulse.

Things started looking up. My wife and family thought that we might be out of the woods. The doctors were even thinking that they might have a miracle man on their hands. But things quickly took a turn for the worse.

I caught a high fever. No one could figure out why. They searched all over my body, both inside and out, to see if they could find any clues. All came to the conclusion that the infection was in my leg. Once again, I was dying. They rushed me into surgery to see if they could clean my infection out and save my life. They told my wife the surgery would take awhile and she should go home and eat or rest. An hour later, my wife received a phone call from the surgeon. He said they couldn't wash or clean out the infection. The infection had gotten too bad and was too far along. The muscle in my lower leg was dead and turned a grayish color. He said that they had to amputate.

Amputate—a word that my wife never expected. And they were calling her and asking permission to perform the amputation. She asked if there was anything else they could do. He gave her a few scenarios, but it all came back to amputation and the only two options possible: "Save his leg or save his life."

She said the very thing that I would have said if I were in her position. "Do whatever you have to do to save my husband's life."

The doctor hung up and proceeded with the amputation.

Originally set to amputate above the knee, one of the nation's renowned amputee surgeons was right next door. Before performing the amputation, the surgeon hesitated and then halted the procedure to ask the all-star amputee surgeon next door his advice. He came in and said that he could save most of the leg. Because God put all the right doctors in all the right places, only a third of my leg was amputated. Instead of being an above-the-knee amputee (which is very difficult to live with), I am a below-the-knee amputee (which all the amputees say isn't an amputee at all . . . kind of rude if you ask me, but it's all in good fun).

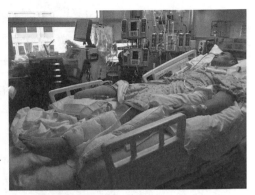

Recovering after the amputation

After my amputation, my fever began to drop. Slow, but steady. By then, they had started slowly bringing me out of my coma. My wife was very nervous about what kind of man I would wake up to be. She wasn't sure if I'd know who she was. The doctors didn't know if I would have brain damage or if the trauma of all of this would change my personality. So when I started coming to, my wife was scared. All of her fears and reservations disappeared when I opened my eyes, looked at her, and winked.

He is strong.

A few days after the incident, while I was still in my coma, something happened in my hospital room that I must not leave out of this chapter.

There was a lady who worked in the ICU. She wasn't a nurse or a doctor but was one of the support staff. Her job was to empty the garbage and the other waste left in the room on a daily basis, which also included human waste. So it was common for her to be going in and out of a patient's room all the time.

One evening while making her regular rounds from room to room, something happened that never happened to her before. She had finished cleaning the room right next to mine and rolled her gear in front of my room. As she began to walk into my room, she was knocked back. Even though my door was open, she was unable to enter my room. Her heart started pounding, and she felt such heat pouring out. Her eyes widened at the sight she was witnessing and slowly stepped away from my room. Turning away from the area, she left the ICU and immediately started looking for one of my family members. The first person she ran across was my mother. She was outside the ICU because it wasn't quite visiting hours yet. As soon as the lady saw my mother, she ran to her and grabbed my mom's hands and squeezed them tight with a grip of sheer terror and utter excitement. She looked my mother straight in the eye and said this:

> "I clean the rooms every day, and when I went to clean your son's room, I couldn't go in. I was knocked back. There were angels all around his bed. They were anointing him. It was so hot in there. Your son's room was too holy for me to enter. It's a holy place. He's being anointed. Your son is going to be fine. He's going to be just fine."

This amazed my mother because even the doctors were certain at that time that I wasn't going to make it. They were expecting me to pass away at any time and were quite confused at why I hadn't died yet.

Never before was there a problem with my room being hot. There were no air-conditioning problems, and I had the same number of machines in my room as all the other patients had. But, beginning that day, for as long as I was a patient in the ICU, my room was hot. The nurses offered to move me into a cooler room, but my wife wouldn't have it. Nobody was going to take her husband out of God's holy place. So in God's holy place I stayed until I left the ICU.

CHAPTER 10

DREAM ON

For our struggle is not against flesh and blood, but ... against the powers of this dark world and against the spiritual forces of evil in the heavenly realms.

~ Ephesians 6:12 NIV

THIS CHAPTER IS VERY DIFFICULT for me to write. I have to rehash some things that were quite terrifying to me. There are still times today when these things haunt me. While being in a coma for twenty days, I was having some pretty graphic and almost unspeakable nightmares. I can't really explain why these things were in my head. I don't know if the drugs the doctors had put me on aided in these nightmares or if there was some kind of spiritual warfare happening in my brain, but I will tell you, I was terrified.

I felt just about every procedure that they were doing to me while I was in my hospital bed. Everything from cutting my stomach open to strapping my wrists to my bed to keep me from pulling out all of my tubes while unconscious.

Once I awoke from my coma (which was medically induced), I had a few pretty bad hallucinations. Those hallucinations were so real, I was scared of the dark and would have panic attacks all through the night for quite some time.

When people say that I've been through hell and back, they don't know how accurate they actually are. While I don't know truly what hell is like, I'm sure that I had a glimpse of it while in a coma. I believe I was engulfed in a battle over my soul. It was spiritual warfare at its highest and I was, unfortunately, aware of the ensuing battle the entire twenty days. Here are four of the worst "nightmares" I had:

THE FISH FACTORY

I had to go to a clinic every day and have dialysis so I would feel good throughout the week. Well, this new clinic was by the water down in Miami, Florida (my hometown). When I got where the address took me, I noticed that the clinic was a big fish warehouse. It looked like a place where they brought the daily catch, cleaned and sold at a wholesale price. Only, they wouldn't clean all the unwanted fish guts from off the ground. There were flies, roaches, and rats all over the place. The place smelled rotten and fishy. The stench was almost unbearable.

Growing up, I would go down to the Florida Keys on the weekends and fish for the weekend. One particular time, I accidently left open a small cooler with a few fish fillets in melted ice inside. Leaving fish in an open cooler in the back seat isn't too bad until the water evaporates and the Miami sun cooks it for three days. The stench was bad enough that

I was unable to drive my car for a while. Even after I took the cooler of fish out of the back seat (I had to use a tool to scrape the melted fillets out of the cooler), the smell lingered in my car for weeks.

In this dream, I didn't want to go into the building, but I knew I had to get the dialysis done or I might die. So I walked in, and the people treated me very nice, all smiles and funny. As I was getting on my designated bed, I felt so thirsty. My tongue started swelling up, and it was hard for me to form words. I managed to utter out a sentence. I said that I was thirsty and asked if I could get some water. With a smile they said they would bring me a glass as soon as they started the procedure. As soon as I laid my body back, my wrists were strapped to the bed. I was feeling a little too vulnerable, so I struggled a little to loosen up the straps, but the more I struggled, the tighter the straps became until the pain was almost unbearable. I decided not to struggle anymore and to wait until someone brought me my water; then I could tell them about the straps. Unfortunately, nobody came.

As I was waiting, I became thirstier and felt my body becoming dehydrated to the point of insanity. To make matters worse, my bed began to levitate off the ground until I was all the way up to the rafters. The warehouse must have been eighty feet tall, and I was up at the ceiling. As soon as I got to the top, I heard screaming and moaning below me. I was alarmed by the sound. The screams and moans were coming from what sounded like little boys. I tried to ignore it for a while, thinking there must be some logical explanation about it. After a few minutes, I just couldn't ignore it any longer. The screams and moans were what sounded like pain and pleas for help. I tried to look over the edge of my bed, but my wrists strapped to the bed prevented me from seeing anything. The screams and moans became louder and louder as the time passed. I finally maneuvered my body so I could see what was going on at the ground below me. What I saw made me scream for help.

Below me, and filling up the whole warehouse, were grown men with all these young boys. They were bringing these boys into the warehouse against the boys' will and tearing their clothes off and raping them. I went crazy at seeing this. I screamed and yelled for help, trying to get out of my straps once more and, again, the straps tightened themselves against my wrists until I saw blood dripping from my wrists and felt the straps were going to pop my hands right off.

After yelling for help to the point of hoarseness, one of the employees of the clinic ran along the rafters and asked me what was wrong. I told him what was going on below me and, with a demon-like look on his face, he told me to ignore it. I was taken aback at the grin curling across his face and his eyes darkening almost black, like a shadow from an eclipse. I told him that I wouldn't just lie here and demanded him to release me right away. At this moment, my feet, which were free from any straps, were tied to the foot of the bed. He then said if I didn't ignore it, I was going to die, and it was going to be today. I tried to play his game and said I was just kidding with him, and I didn't care what was going on in the warehouse. He laughed and loosened my straps. I asked if I could use the computer. He consented and brought me an old laptop. I noticed it had a zip drive in the port that had all the camera footage of the warehouse. The man was walking away until he remembered he left the zip drive in the laptop he let me use. As he turned and started running back toward me with an even more grotesque demon face than before, I put the zip drive in my mouth and swallowed it.

He jumped on me and, with a deep and paralyzing screech, he said I made a big mistake. He took my pillow and started smothering me with it. I couldn't get any oxygen in my lungs and didn't have enough strength to free myself from his grasp. Try as I might, I couldn't get free, and I started fading fast. Darkness turned into white spots, which turned black again. Finally, my struggle was no more.

That was the first nightmare.

IRAQ

Suddenly, I was getting off a plane in the middle of the night in Iraq. Walking through deserted city streets was a very eerie feeling. Sand and empty clay structures trying to pass as buildings outlined the black horizon as flickering street lights illuminated the dirt roads beneath them. This town could be a perfect location to film a post apocalyptic movie. Walking with my rucksack, listening to the sound of my boots pounding the ground beneath me and a single mutt barking in the far off distance, I had a sinking feeling that I was being watched.

My orders were to report to a command in the center of town. Walking up to an old and broken down building, I noticed my nose was throbbing. A tube of some sort was hanging out of one of my nostrils. Every step I took and every move of my head was pain. When I walked into the workshop, my commanding officer met me with a disarming smile. I found it odd that she had such a warm attitude despite the hopeless environment she was in command of.

The officer gave me the tour of the workshop and introduced me to the enlisted men and women under her charge whom I was going to be working with. She told me she had to go brief the Pentagon and announced to the crew that nobody was to mess with me while she was away. She said the tube in my nose wasn't ready to be taken out and she was the only one who knew how to do it. (Why I had a tube in my nose in my dream, I didn't know.) Everyone gave a "Yes, ma'am," and she left.

As she left, I noticed two soldiers looking at each other in an unsettling way. As they started walking toward me, their faces started to deform in a way that looked between a pig's face and a clown's. Their skin turned costume makeup white and their nostrils started turning into snouts as their smiles grew three times its former size. I tried backing up, but I was cornered on the far side of the workshop. They grabbed me and pinned me on a table, causing the tools lying there to bury themselves into my back. One of the soldiers took a pair of needle nose pliers and shoved it in my nostril where the tube was running through as the other soldier pinned my arms to the table. As the one was pulling the tube out of my nostril, the taste of blood was in my throat. The warmth of it was running into my right eye and down my cheek. Once again, I was suffocating, drowning in my own blood. I imagine the pain of the tube being pulled out is what it would feel like if my brain was being pulled out of my nose.

After the tube was pulled out, they got some copper wiring that was resting on the table, unraveled it, and began shoving it through my other nostril. The pain of the wire being pulled in was even worse than the tube being pulled out. As hard as I struggled, it was in vain. I couldn't break free.

As I was about to black out from oxygen deprivation, they let me go, and I rolled off the table. Desperate for air, I began spitting up blood onto the dusty floor of the workshop while gasping for the air I was denied just moments ago. Laughter erupted as I got up and ran out into the streets. I tried to run, but my feet were heavy, as if I was running in waist deep water.

I heard gunshots in the distance. Despite running the other direction from the gunfire, the popping of the rounds of ammunition was getting louder and louder. I knew somebody was coming after me, either the terrorists or the soldiers, neither of which I wanted to see. As I turned off into an alley, the last thing I remembered before blacking out was a loud gunshot and two pairs of familiar eyes.

That was the second nightmare.

TIMES SQUARE

Air Force One was flying out of the Middle East with newly-elected for the second time, President Barrack Obama. (I predicted he would win a second term before I was shot.) Also on the plane was my pregnant wife Susan, Jason, and I. A few hours into our flight, the plane was hit by a rocket and started to dive at a rapid pace. The only area that we could land in was Times Square in New York City. As we braced for impact, I grabbed my wife's hand and told her that everything was going to be fine. I didn't want her to worry.

The plane crash-landed in one piece. Except a few bumps and bruises, everyone on board was safe and relieved to be alive. As we prepared to exit the aircraft, we heard a loud commotion outside. I looked out a window and saw what seemed to be a small city of Somali pirates armed with AK-47s and machetes. The pilot assured us that the plane could not be breached and, as long as we stayed inside the plane, we'd be safe.

Looking out the cockpit windows, I saw a massacre taking place. The Americans, or what was left of them anyway, were being killed and mutilated in front of my eyes. The Somali pirates who weren't murdering Americans were working on the plane's fuselage. The machetes ricocheting off the metal structure and gunshots ripping through the fiberglass walls were deafening. A few of the terrorists were making headway with one of the doors damaged in the crash.

It was clear to the pilot the pirates were going to get through the door, so he quickly took President Obama into the cockpit and locked the cockpit door behind them, leaving my family and I to fend for ourselves.

I kissed my wife and told her I loved her and hugged my son. I put them in one of the bathrooms and told them to lock the door and not to come out for any reason. As soon as my wife and son secured themselves in the bathroom, the fuselage door was ripped open and the Somalis came pouring in.

I managed to hit and knock out a few until I was overtaken and slammed against the wall. One of the Somali pirates easily kicked open the bathroom door and grabbed my wife. He threw her to the slew of other terrorists as they yelled in triumph. It was the sound of wild animals that are about to devour their prey. They also grabbed my son and both of them disappeared from my view as they were carried out of the plane and into the streets of Times Square.

I yelled, screamed, and cried. I tried to move, but I was paralyzed. My job was to protect them, and I failed.

That was the third nightmare.

THE MONKEY HYBRID

As I lay in my hospital bed, a friend and his wife paid me a visit. It was dark in my room. The only light was a soft orange glow that came from a candle on the opposite side of the room.

My friend and his wife had made an emergency trip from Nicaragua where they are missionaries. They told me they needed some of my hair from my stomach so they can clone some babies. Having complete trust in them, I said I'd be happy to help and signed the consent form for them. The moment I signed the form, a group of doctors rushed into my room and started slowly pulling out all my stomach hair from my sternum down. The pain was excruciating. I tried to get them to stop, but they wouldn't relent. Once again, I was strapped to the bed and couldn't free my hands. It was the same bed from the fish factory, but it was soiled with blood from my wrists, dust from Iraq, and gunpowder from the Somali pirates.

After all the hair on my stomach was gone, the doctors left. My friend and his wife handed me two newborns I helped to clone. They placed them on my chest and they explained to me what they really were. I looked at them and saw a grotesque monkey-human hybrid, like an experiment gone wrong from the Island of Doctor Moreau. They were deformed and hairless. Not quite a monkey, but not quite human. The two mutants looked up at me and gave a crooked smile.

As I tried to pull away from them, my friend congratulated me and told me they were the first batch, and they were mine.

This was, by far, the strangest of dreams that I had. I can still feel their cold hands crawling up my chest. I truly believe I was engulfed in spiritual warfare.

My waking moments weren't much different. My hallucinations haunted me throughout the night and consumed my thoughts throughout the day. The sounds of gunshots right outside my hospital room window kept me up at night. I would yell for the nurses and tell them someone was being shot right under my window, but they assured me there were no gunshots. While lying in bed awake, I saw a shadowy figure sitting in the chair that was located in the corner of the room. He never looked at me. He would just stare out the window with his feet propped up on the window sill. When the daylight came, he would disappear. Every night, I called the attending nurse and asked if there was a man sitting in the corner. No matter which nurse was working that night, the answer was always the same: "No. No one here but me."

Every night, a voodoo lady would show up in the ICU. She had skin as dark as the night and thin dreadlocks hanging down past her shoulders. Her clothes looked more like dirty rags dangling off her bony body. I would watch her run into people's rooms and terrorize them. I know this because I would hear yells and screams in the rooms that she entered. I was always scared that she would come into my room eventually, but she never did. She would just walk up to my door and stare at me through the window, like a kid looking at a display in a toy store window. Her eyes would be wide with want, almost like her appetite wouldn't be fulfilled until she had me. But she never came in. I felt my heart stop every time she came to my door. I didn't want to move. I figured if I was still enough, she wouldn't see me.

Night after night, I would get panic attacks. I'd wake up and feel like I was being asphyxiated. I called the nurse to let her know I couldn't breathe. She would medicate me and put an oxygen mask on me. I felt better until the meds wore off, and then I would hear the gunshots again . . . or see the voodoo lady outside my door.

My days were long, but my nights were longer. When visiting hours were over for the night, I would grab my mother and plead with her not to leave. She later told me my eyes would get really wide and I kept looking around and over to the corner. I was truly afraid of the dark.

CHAPTER 11

LIFE SUPPORT

All of you together are Christ's body, and each of you is a part of it.

~ 1 Corinthians 12:27 NLT

MY MOTHER AND FATHER ATTENDED University Baptist Church (UBC) before I was born. They went because my mother's parents went, so naturally, when I was born, I went to UBC. I'm a "third-generation churchgoer," if you will. I've been blessed to have a group of guys in my class who loved the Lord as much as I did. Those guys became more than friends to me. They became my brothers. They were the kind of guys, even if years would go by without speaking to each other, the second we got back together, it was like we hadn't missed a day. We grew up in the church together. After Sunday school on Sunday morning, we'd walk to Kentucky Fried Chicken and then come back to the church and play football in the fellowship hall until choir started later that evening. As Garth Brooks once wrote, "Blood is thicker than water, but love is thicker than blood." We loved each other, and we were always there if a situation arose. Their wives became my sisters, and their kids became my nephews and nieces.

When the word reached Miami that I had been shot, time ceased to exist for them. Everything in their busy lives was put on hold as they fell to their knees and begged the Lord to save me. Chris, who lives in Nicaragua as a missionary and is one of my closest friends, got up on his roof with his wife to pray because he wanted to get as close to God as he could, asking the Lord to heal me.

Within about twenty minutes of hearing about the shooting, thousands upon thousands were praying on my behalf.

Because I grew up in church, praying for one another is not a strange or uncommon thing to me. We, as the body of Christ, are called to pray. If one of us is hurt, then the whole body is hurt. I was lucky enough to be a part of a thriving church in Miami that hungered for a lasting and intimate relationship with the Lord. The power of prayer is a real thing. I am convinced that because of all the people praying on my behalf, I am alive today.

The Lord honors those who pray faithfully, and God became very real to many that night of October 17, 2012. No longer was the Lord a distant deity who performed miracles many years ago. He was, and is, a God who has the power to move mountains, and because of a call to arms by my brothers and sisters, the people of UBC prayed faithfully. I tell people today that my God is the Mountain Maker. He is the One who tells the ocean that it can go this far, but no farther. If He is the Creator of this world, He surely can save a little piece of nothing like me, if He wishes.

UBC wasn't the only group praying for me. Derek, my older brother, works for Upward Sports, a Christian sports ministry that has leagues all around the world. I've had the opportunity to be close to the organization and the people who work for Upward, and it has been such a blessing to me. The people there have a real heart for the Lord and the mission of the organization. When Derek found out what happened, he quickly called the founder of Upward, Caz, and told him what had occurred. It wasn't long before the people of Upward in Spartanburg, South Carolina, and around the world were praying for me as well.

I didn't realize how many people were praying for me until months after the initial incident. During that time, I was fighting for my life and doing some praying of my own. But every prayer that was prayed on my behalf was needed because I couldn't make it alone. I needed all the help I could get, and most importantly, I needed the Lord in my corner.

My sister-in-law, Ginger, figured out a way to give everybody updates without sending mass texts. She started a CaringBridge page online.

CaringBridge is a blog website that allows people to get regular updates as well as leave words of encouragement. It also allows people to donate to the family to help provide for any needs the family may have in their tragic situation.

Because Ginger started the page, many people felt they were right in the hospital room with me. My incident became more real to them, and they felt the hurt when I made a turn for the worse and the joy when a miracle occurred during a procedure. The website gave detailed situations for which people could pray. So when people were praying for me, they prayed specifically and not generally.

In all, over 73,000 people visited my CaringBridge page, and more than four times that number were praying for me through Facebook and mass e-mails.

Within a day of the shooting, over twenty of my friends and family came to the hospital to support my wife and son. Friends from South America to South Florida would come for

My sister, brother, and I at the VA hospital

sometimes just a few hours to be there for Susan and whatever she or the family needed.

My family and friends knew the first few days were crucial to my survival. On day two, my dad, mom, sister, and brother joined hands in a circle and prayed to the Lord. My dad led the prayer, and what he prayed stunned all in the circle. He prayed for the Lord to have mercy on me and allow me to come out of this alive. But then he said, "Lord, if you want him, take him."

I'm sure you could have heard a pin drop in that room. I can't imagine how hard that must have been for him to say. I have a son, and I don't know if I could say that to the Lord. But this shows spiritual maturity because, ultimately, I don't belong to my dad, my mom, or even my wife. I belong to the Lord.

My mother, of course, did not approve of what my dad said. She broke the circle and started crying, saying, "No, no, no. Not my son. You can't have him."

I feel her words were a completely appropriate response at the time. I haven't nor do I ever want to be in the shoes of my parents. The difficulty that they had to face those first twenty days must have been near unbearable. Every day, they were certain that the doctors were going to come in and tell them that I was gone. As I was dying on the outside, my family was dying on the inside.

My cousin Jack flew in from Texas, slept on the floor in my house, and spent the day at the hospital only to look at me through the window for about ten minutes. Then, he got back on a plane and flew back to Texas. That's love.

My brother-in-law, Kenton, was at a Bible study at Argyle Church of Christ the night I was shot. I had gone with him a couple of times before and had met the pastors (Ken and Nathan) and some of the members of the congregation. Kenton's wife, Diane (Susan's sister), came rushing into the church sanctuary and grabbed Kenton. When she whispered in his ear what happened, he sprang up and they ran to the already running car and rushed to the hospital. Ken, as he was teaching the night's lesson, thought it was strange, until he found out what happened. Once Pastor Ken announced my being shot, the entire Argyle congregation prayed for my life. They covered me in prayer and prayed constantly, even to this day. Since then, Pastor Ken and I have developed a very close relationship. I also had the privilege to speak to the congregation about the incident and how God moved and has shown His glory through this incident.

In the Bible, James 5:14 says, "Is anyone among you sick? Let them call the elders of the church to pray over them and anoint them with oil in the name of the Lord."

We as Christians are the body of Christ and are called to stick together and pray for each other in times of trouble. We are all broken. We are all "sick." That's why we come together as a church—so that we can pray for one another. If I hadn't been plugged into a church down in Miami or here in Jacksonville, I might not have gotten the prayer that was much needed in my most desperate hour. Who knows what the outcome might have been?

If I survived the gunshot wound, the next nine months would be some very dark and tough times. I wouldn't have my fellow brothers and sisters in Christ to lean on when I needed them the most. There are many of us that have kind of swept church to the side because we like sleeping in on the weekends or think that we don't need to attend to have a relationship with our God. And, in a way, that may be true. But when your life is suddenly turned upside down, it's the church that will be there to turn it right again. You may think you might not need them now but, honestly, now is when you need church more than ever. Because you never know what the next ten minutes might bring.

Even Jesus got weary, and when He was weary, He leaned on His disciples. Because of University Baptist Church, Upward Sports, First Baptist Church Spartanburg, Argyle Church of Christ, and Caringbridge.org, I had prayer, support, and love. My wife didn't feel alone. My son was well taken care of, and my family and friends had a great support system.

I also need to mention my mother-in-law. When Susan heard the news of my situation, she rushed as fast as she could to be by my side. And as she was rushing to be by my side, her mother was rushing to be by hers. From

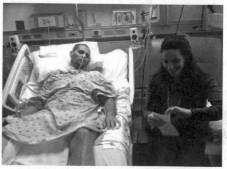

Susan never left my side

October 17 to February 17, Denise (Susan's mother) stood by her side and became Susan's rock. When Susan collapsed from grief, Denise was there to catch her. She became another mom to Jason and later Stella. My mother-in-law put her life on hold for four months until I was able to come home. Denise was a great example of sacrifice and what it means to be a servant. As some people look at me as their hero, I look at her as mine. Denise protected my wife and kids while I was incapacitated and unable to come home, and for this, I'll forever be grateful.

Although I am done with all my surgeries and have been feeling much better for some time now, I still update CaringBridge on a regular basis. For so long, people heard so much bad news about my health with very little good news; now that I'm better, I'm trying to balance the scale. I'd like a little more good news and hopefully no more bad news.

CHAPTER 12

I CAN DO ALL THINGS; THE LONG ROAD BACK TO NORMAL

"Survival can be summed up in three words
—NEVER GIVE UP.
That's the heart of it really. Just keep trying."

~ Bear Grylls

FEBRUARY 28, 2013, THE REEBOK-SPONSORED "Spartan Race" was coming to Miami to challenge the locals to an obstacle course that spans about eight miles. Rope climbs, open water swims, and "Spartans" with jousting poles are just a few challenges in the eighty-minute course. My mother called me and said that she felt that she wanted to pursue this crazy venture (my mother is in her 60s ... don't tell anybody) and wanted to know if I'd run it with her. I was 205 lbs, at the time and didn't do much cardio. I was strictly a weight lifter and didn't have much of a desire to run an obstacle course, let alone one that was eight miles long.

After some prodding and sales pitching by my sweet mother, I agreed to do it with her as well as her husband and his daughter. Signing up for the race in March of 2012 gave me roughly eleven months to train and get my mind right.

As the months flew by, I was getting more and more excited about running the race. It had been a long time since I set a personal goal. The closer the race got, the more intense my workouts became. No longer was I strictly in the gym. My workout consisted of hours of both weight lifting as well as functional exercises out in a field or on a track. Push-ups, pull ups, dips, and burpees were as frequent in my life as breathing. I dropped my weight from 205 lbs. to 192 lbs. and upped my strength as well. For example, my bench press went from a 275 lb. max. to 315 lb. max. I could honestly say I was in the best shape of my life. In fact, I talked to my dad on the phone that evening before getting out of my car to meet my client and told him that I was the strongest I had ever been. About two hours before talking with him, I benched 315 pounds, five times on my fifth set. This was very significant because it was a weight which I never thought I would ever reach. I had no way of knowing that, ten minutes later, someone would press the reset button, and all that I'd accomplished would be wiped from existence. It's amazing to think that all the training wasn't preparing me for the Spartan Race, but to save my life. The doctors said if I hadn't been in such good shape, I wouldn't have survived all the surgeries.

The first thing I remember after waking up twenty days later in the hospital was how hot my body was. I was soaked with sweat and wanted to get my feet out from under the sheets. I knew that most body heat is released from the head and feet. As I pulled on my sheets,

I successfully freed my left foot from the confines of the sheets but couldn't get my right foot out. No matter how much sheet I pulled, nothing came out. At one point, I had all of the sheets crumbled up on my chest and was looking at only one foot, but still couldn't put it together. Now, when you wake up from being asleep for twenty days, you're not all there in the head. There is confusion and a lot of drugs involved. I was VERY confused, to say the least. I kept trying to get out of bed, but everyone forced me to stay put. I kept telling the nurses that I was fine and could transfer to a chair, no problem, but I was forced to stay in bed. It wasn't until about a week later that I saw my reflection in a window and noticed I didn't have a foot.

My missing foot was really the least of my problems. Because of lying in bed for so long, my body was feeding on itself. Most of my muscles were gone. My remaining strength was exerted to move my limbs and turn my head, even though moving my head, in itself, was a challenge. My weight went from a strong 192 lbs. to a frail 132 lbs. I wouldn't be able to look myself in the mirror for another two months, but when I did, I didn't recognize the skeleton that was looking back at me. It would take seven months before I finally looked like myself again.

You would think that the weakest I had ever been was when I took my first gasps of breath as a baby, but you'd be wrong. At least, as a baby, I could breathe on my own. I was hooked up to a breathing machine for weeks after I woke up from the coma. I remember my wife being so happy that I was alive (and awake) that she would give me long kisses on the mouth every few minutes. As sweet as it was, she had no idea that she was suffocating me, and I didn't have the heart to tell her. I didn't really understand why she was so happy to see me. In my mind, I saw her yesterday. I wouldn't find out until two months later that I was in a coma for twenty days and that my survival had baffled all the doctors.

Because of two collapsed lungs and lying still for almost a month, it was very hard for me to speak. My first few weeks were a whispering slur. My words weren't coming out the way I wanted them to. Whispering a single sentence would take most of my energy. If Susan didn't understand it the first time, I'd have to regroup and try again. It was a very frustrating time. Not to mention the feeding tube

The moment I discovered my leg was gone

up my nose and down to my stomach and the tube that was stuck in my throat right under my Adam's apple, helping me breathe. Because of all the time with tubes and trauma to my body, my vocal cords were so weak that I could barely make a sound that wasn't just air slurring off my lips.

When I was shot, the bullet shredded my right kidney. Because of the trauma to my kidney and my body as a whole, my remaining kidney completely shut down. If you don't have kidney function, you don't live very long. So for the next two months, I would have to undergo four hours of dialysis on a daily basis, one of the most uncomfortable experiences I've ever had. For those who don't know what dialysis is, let me describe it. They basically suck your blood out and filter/clean it in a big machine and pump it back into your body. Because your blood leaves your body, it cools off, and when put back into your body, you're chilled to the bone. The dialysis patient can't get warm no matter how many blankets you drape over him. I was very thankful to the Lord the day I didn't need dialysis anymore. My remaining kidney eventually began working again. I was extremely happy when I was told that I'd never see the dialysis machine again.

After the bullet shredded my right kidney, it continued to travel down my body and ripped through my colon. Because of the extensive damage, the surgeons had to remove a third of it. Since my body had to heal before my waste could travel through what was left of my colon, and because my body couldn't take another surgery, I had an ileostomy, which came with complementary bags. Let me tell you what I know of ileostomies. It's basically a removal of a part of your intestine and leaving you with a part of your intestine showing, called a "stoma." Since some of your intestine is hanging out of your stomach, you have to attach a bag to it because your feces is constantly flowing out of it. Yes, you poop all day. You have to constantly check the bag as well because if it gets too full, the bag will explode. As you well know, people pass gas a good part of the day, and so did I, except, I was passing gas in a bag that acted much like a balloon when full of gas. So I would have to periodically "burp" the bag to let the gas out (I just gagged).

Let's play a game. Think of the most pleasant scent you can think of. Do you have it? Now think of the exact opposite of that smell and multiply it by ten. That's how bad it stunk! I was relieved when the doctors said that it was only temporary. I wouldn't get it reversed until six months down the road. To tell you the truth, it was six months too long.

Out of all the issues I have had due to the shooting, the ileostomy was the hardest for me. Even the surgery to reverse it knocked me down. There was so much pain when I had it reversed and, unfortunately, I had to go back into the hospital two weeks after the reversal because of an infection that caused a grapefruit sized abscess in my abdomen. It's very common with these procedures. Just for the record, everything is working like it did before.

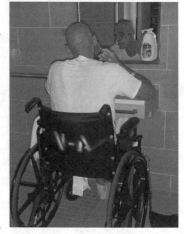

My motor skills were knocked off kilter because of the shooting. When I woke up, I couldn't put my two pointer fingers together. When they asked me to clap, I clapped my hands together one out of every four attempts. Picking up a pen from the tray was a huge challenge in itself. My wife would have to

I had to learn how to shave again

lead my hand to grab an item off the bed table. I was never a good handwriter before the incident, but to put a pen to a piece of paper after was laughable. There were times that I had to sign a military document or a hospital consent form, and all I could do was draw two crooked horizontal lines. I'd like to see what it looks like now that I can write again. It's probably pretty embarrassing. It took me a few months to start feeling comfortable with my handwriting. Writing was such a simple task that I took for granted. Now, what an accomplishment just to write my name!

As the days turned to weeks, I improved little by little. Then out of the blue, some complication would send me back into surgery. There was one area on my body (my groin area), where a fem to fem bypass was located, that kept filling up with fluid. Evidently, there was a pocket of space left when they patched me up the first time, allowing excess fluid in my body to "collect" in this pocket. It expanded more each day. It got so big at one point that there was what looked like a mango-sized pocket of fluid on the inside of my upper leg, which was extremely painful and uncomfortable, to say the least.

In six days, I had three "wash out" surgeries in the same area. One of the procedures included a "muscle flap." They took my muscle, cut it, and moved it on top of my artificial vein under the pocket of fluid. Not only did this halt my rehab improvement, but I lost a lot of what I learned just days before. I compare it to climbing a steep mountainside. I was climbing to the top, doing very well, and then I would lose my footing (no pun intended) and slide almost all the way down before catching myself again. It was so frustrating that when the doctors came in and told me they had to go in for a third time, I thanked them, waited until they left the room, and started to cry. My body kept breaking down. I remember turning to my mother, who was visiting me at the time, and saying to her, "I feel like my body wants to die, but my mind won't let it." I might have even been right. My mind wanted to live, long before my body got on board with the idea. Because of the

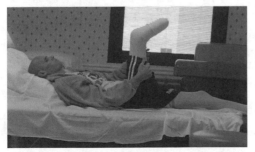

three surgeries in the same area, the lymph nodes in my left leg were damaged and caused me to be diagnosed with lymphedema.

Walking was another feat that I thought near impossible for about three

Most of my rehab had to be completed on my back

and a half months. My body had gone through so much trauma that I could stand for only about fifteen seconds before blacking out. My first day in physical therapy in the Tampa Veterans Hospital (James A. Haley), I tried to show off by standing up between the horizontal bars to walk on a basic prosthetic. Not only did I black out, but I threw up my fine hospital breakfast in one of the trash cans, smelling up the whole place. What an impression I made.

Rehab in the Tampa VA hospital

Once I was strong enough to stand upright for a decent amount of time, the challenge of taking a few steps with an artificial bottom third of a leg was a challenge all by itself. I would begin with just standing with a walker, then take baby steps with the walker, then bigger steps, and finally travel some distance. When I say some distance, I mean forty feet or so.

After I conquered the walker, I would do the whole thing over again with crutches, and then forearm crutches, then two canes, one cane, and finally, without any help at all. Each stage was two or more weeks at a time. Once mastered, I graduated to the next "crutch," but only if I was perfect with the previous. It was a very frustrating time for me. Only a few months earlier, I was in the best shape of my life, but now I couldn't even stand on my own without blacking out and throwing up. I couldn't get through this without the strength and power of my Lord and Savior, Jesus Christ. Philippians 4:13 says, "I can do all things through Christ who strengthens me."

This verse played through my head the entire time I was rehabbing and trying to get back to "normal." Contrary to popular belief, I didn't look at this as some kind of depressing, life-ending tragedy. To me, this was a challenge. I had been in the best shape of my life. I had reached my goal only to be told to go back to the starting line. Now, to reach the goal once again would be twice as sweet as my previous victory.

April 14, 2014 was the next Spartan Race in Miami. I hoped I'd be to the point in my fitness and rehab to be able to run it. Unfortunately, I have just started being able to run. But another opportunity has arisen in my life.

Some months back, I was contacted by Navy Wounded Warrior Safe Harbor, an organization for coordinating the non-medical care of seriously wounded, ill, and injured sailors and coast guardsmen, and providing resources and support to their families. One thing that falls under "non-medical care" is in the form of reintegration activities such as sports and athletics. Sandra was my case worker in the Tampa Veterans Hospital as well as a Safe Harbor representative. She introduced me to the organization and what it had to offer. At the time, I was in so much pain and was so exhausted from hours of rehab that I didn't want to hear a thing about sports. Just thinking of the word tired me out. About a year later, I was ready for it.

I started feeling better and stronger. My energy was coming back, and I was looking for a challenge outside the hospital. Sandra got back in touch with me and told me about an upcoming competition in Hawaii named "The Wounded Warrior Pacific Invitational." I registered and took a week off from my physical therapy to fly to Hawaii. (I know! Poor me!)

I was amazed to see how many other amputees were in the competition. I felt a real bond with these guys. As an amputee, I felt alone in Jacksonville. I knew people looked at me when I was walking through the mall; I was seen as a guy without a leg and not as a regular person. It made me extremely self-conscious. In Hawaii, we all stuck together and looked out for each other like a real brotherhood. Because of competing, I became more confident and less self-conscious.

As my first time to attempt anything athletic without the lower part of my leg, I had no idea what event I wanted to compete in. I couldn't compete in track because I couldn't run yet, and my lack of flexibility in my leg hindered me from doing much else. So I tried my hand in Shot Put and Discus. Because I had reached only about sixty percent of my health physically, I embarrassed myself in the field events. I laughed it off because I knew this was my first time and I was only going to get better.

On the blocks at the Warrior Games

I saw that there was a swim meet that I could sign up for as well. I was always good in the water and, as you know, initially came into the Navy as a rescue swimmer, so I decided to sign up. I competed in the 50 meter freestyle, 100 meter freestyle, and 50 meter backstroke. I was surprised when I took first place in all three events, even beating out most guys who had both legs. Because I did so well in my heats, "Team Navy" (Go Navy!) selected me to compete in the 200 meter relay. We took the silver only because our anchor

I took two bronze medals at the Warrior Games in 2014

was fatigued from just finishing his 100-meter freestyle heat.

After competing in the water in Hawaii, I was hooked! It was the first time I had ever competed in swimming. Since then, I've been working hard in the pool every week. I have a new goal to attain. I want to win the gold medal in the 2016 Paralympics Games in Rio, Brazil. I'm working hard every day to make "Team U.S.A." Texas Regional Games, Warrior Games Trials, and the Warrior Games are just a few competitions that I'll be swimming in to try and make my times faster and impress the U.S.A. Paralympic coaches.

I've found that setting goals in each chapter of your life is of upmost importance. Even if you don't attain your goal, it keeps you striving to better yourself on a daily basis. The Lord might not have a plan for me to participate in a future Paralympics, and that's okay. But I'm going to train for it until He closes the door—if He closes the door. Until then, let's go do some good.

CHAPTER 13

FROM THREE OF A KIND TO A FULL HOUSE

"Other things may change us, but we start and end with family."
~ Anthony Brandt

AS FAR BACK AS I could remember, I wanted a family of my own. I remember wanting a wife, some kids, and a dog living in a nice, relatively quiet house. The desire became stronger after my parents divorced. When my teen years turned into my early twenties, I was a little concerned I wouldn't find my wife, and I sure wasn't going to settle for "good enough." When my early twenties turned into my late twenties, I was almost sure the Lord didn't have a wife planned for my future. But I stayed faithful and refused to settle for simply any girl who would bat her eyes at me. Then, at the ripe old age of twenty-eight and three quarters (at least that's how I felt), I met Susan, and from the moment I saw her, I knew she was going to be my wife. I knew if we weren't going to be married to one another, it wasn't going to be because of anything I did. She would have to break it off with me. Luckily, she felt the same way, so, at the riper older

Susan and I

age of thirty (November 28, 2009), Susan became my wife. She looked stunning, breathtaking, and, me . . . I looked . . . eh.

You know the saying, "Marry me, marry my family"? It's true with pets as well. I've always been a big dog guy. I've been raised with Golden Labrador Retrievers. Baffin was the first, and Chestnut (Chessy) was the second. They both lived to about twelve years of age. So when Susan told me she had a white cotton ball of a dog named Jessie, I was a bit taken aback. Jessie is a Bichon Frisé, white and puffy and with that annoying little dog bark. To me, little dogs were too close to being cats, and I don't like cats. I'm sorry, cat lovers; allergies or something.

Jessie must have known I didn't care for him too much, because he was dead set on winning me over. When I would sit on the couch, he would jump up and lay right on my lap and watch TV with me. If I got up and walked around the house, he wouldn't leave my side. And if I was in the kitchen, he'd lie in his little doggy bed and just stare at me. There is only so much little puppy dog eyes that a man can take before he falls in love with a canine. Well, this is what happened to me. So when I was told Jessie was going to be my "son," I was more than happy to adopt him as my own.

Susie, Jessie, and I had some great times together in our little townhouse in Jacksonville for a good year or so. We would go on walks on nature trails in some preserve or go to Bruster's Ice Cream and get Jessie some doggy ice cream when we felt the urge. I know, nauseating, right? Then one day, Susan took a pregnancy test, and the results came up positive. The doctor confirmed it a week later, and we started to prepare for our first child—I mean, human child.

Susan while pregnant

A few months later, we found out the sex. My heart jumped out of my chest when the doctor said it was a boy. I fought my hardest to keep the tears from flowing. I was so happy to be having a boy. I got in my car with a huge grin on my face and began driving home. About half way home, I turned on the radio, and that's when the tears fell. Brad Paisley's song "Anything Like Me" was playing. It's a song about Mr. Paisley finding out the sex of his son and thinking about if he's going to be anything like his daddy. That song was so very relevant to me, and so cry-worthy. I almost had to pull the car over because I couldn't see though my tears. Just in case you aren't sure, these were tears of joy.

June 6 came, and my little boy was born: Jason Anthony Parks. He was breached, so they rushed Susan in for an emergency c-section. I was nervous but all was well, and both child and mother were healthy. After Jason was born, I followed him and the nurse to the newborn room where he got his first shots and official weight, and I had to sign the birth certificate. I remember holding him in my arms for the first time and just staring at him. Although there were a few nurses in the room with us, it was as if the world didn't exist. It was just me and my boy. He was looking up at me with his deep blue eyes, and I remember thinking that I've never loved anything as much as I loved him.

After a few days, Susan, Jason, and I were discharged, and we took the normally five-minute drive home. I say normally because this particular time took us twice as long because I refused to go the speed limit. I was actually going five miles under the speed limit. People didn't like it, but I didn't care. We would have gotten in the car sooner if I could have figured out the car seat thing on my own.

Men, you think it's embarrassing to ask for directions? It's not nearly as embarrassing as asking how to put your child in the car. Not a good start to fatherhood. That night, I put Jason in his crib and placed my hand on his chest and prayed to the Lord. I asked the Lord to bless him and protect him through all of Jason's days. I asked that the Lord would be with me and to help me show Jesus to Jason. I lifted him up to the Lord and told Him that Jason was His child and asked Him to help me raise him in a godly way.

Jason has been such a blessing to us. He really fills our life with such joy. This kid is a trip! He makes us laugh all the time. There are things he does I have to discipline him for, but I have to turn my back after I carry out the punishment because I'm starting to laugh. Even when he's bad, he's great. Susan and I love him so much.

Jason was and is such a good baby/child; naturally we planned on having another. Almost a year after Jason was born; Susan's pregnancy test came up positive again. We were having another baby. You would think if a couple had a boy first, they would want a girl next. We were not that couple. Both Susan and I wanted only boys. Susan wanted to be the only girl in the house (Jessie the dog is a male) and I wanted

Jason to have a little brother like my brother had me. My brother and I have a great relationship and always have. I wanted Jason to have the same thing.

When the day came to find out the sex, we were all prepared to hear the words, "It's a little boy," so we were a bit surprised when we heard, "It's a girl." Susan didn't take it nearly as badly as I did. On the contrary, Susan was excited. She would later say she was secretly hoping for a girl. I, on the other hand, almost had a panic attack. I automatically fast forwarded to when she will be sixteen. All the boys I'd have to scare. All the gray hair I will get worrying about her. All the sleepless nights thinking about what's going on in her life. And the wedding!!! Having to give her away?!?! Good grief!! It took me a few weeks to settle down. Yes, it took me two weeks to stop worrying about what might happen in sixteen or even eighteen years. As the months passed by, I got more and more excited, wondering what she was going to look like, how she was going to act, who she will be. There was no warning that in month seven of Susan's pregnancy, a life-changing event would happen, and we would never be the same again.

When Susan heard about me being shot, she went into shock. She was still functioning and all, but she wasn't sleeping or eating. Many were concerned this could hurt the baby's development, possibly killing the baby. The doctors put her on high risk and told her she needed to get some rest. Sleep was the last thing that Susan cared about. The doctors didn't worry about the baby when it came to Susan eating. They said that the baby would take all her nutrients from Susan. Basically, Susan would starve to death before the baby would. This wasn't good news either.

Susan's c-section was scheduled for December 13 in Jacksonville. Unfortunately, I was transferred to James A. Haley Veterans Hospital in

Tampa, Florida, on December 4 and was too weak to travel back and forth. I missed my little girl being born. Nevertheless, Stella Marie Parks came into this world beautiful and healthy. I didn't see her until six days later when my stunner

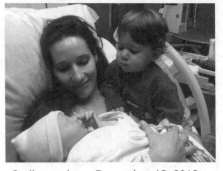

Stella was born December 13, 2012

of a wife hopped in the car and drove four hours to surprise me. Not only was I completely surprised to see Susan in Tampa so soon after the delivery, but I was so overwhelmed to see my little girl. I took Stella into my arms and just stared at her. I whispered to her that I was her daddy and I would die before seeing her harmed. I told her I will always protect her and will love her more than any other man could. Then I told her that she was grounded until she goes to college.

To be honest, I didn't feel that instant bond and love for her like I did with Jason. I think it was because I wasn't there for the delivery. This is yet another example of something that the gunman took from me. I wouldn't develop that bond and love for my daughter for a few months.

About a month after I returned home, I was upstairs in Jason's room with everybody. Stella was on the floor, lying on her back. Jason was playing with a train set, and Susan was getting Jason's clothes laid out for the next day. I started putting my whiskers on Stella's bare ribs and tickling her, kind of like I was eating her. She smiled a lot, so I kept doing it. A few moments later, she belted out a laugh. It was her first laugh, and I was the cause of it. I fell in love with her right then and there. This was exactly what I needed. I needed a moment with her I could call my own, like I had with Jason in the newborn room. That was our moment, and my feelings for her were never the same again.

Unlike Jason, my little wrestling buddy whom I allow to learn stuff the hard way, I have had this security mentality with Stella. I just want to coddle her in my arms and protect her from everything. I don't want

Meeting my daughter for the first time

her to feel pain. I don't want her heart to break. I don't want her to be upset. I know if she's in my arms, she'll forever be safe. She is the most precious little person that I've ever known. I love my son, but there's something about my little girl. I was crazy to just want boys. I'm so happy the Lord knows what He's doing and gave me a little girl. I get so excited during the day when I know I'm going to get to see her soon. She's so pretty and sweet. I love my little Stella.

My family went from three of us to five in a hurry. To tell you the truth, we haven't ruled out having another child. Susan is an incredible pregnant woman. She doesn't ache; no morning sickness, no mood swings. I never saw her fatigued. Our kids are so good as well, and I credit this to Susan and her balance of discipline and grace. We've had such a great experience during the child-bearing stage that we are leaning toward having a third. Jessie probably won't like that, but he'll get over it.

There is a Bible verse that's on the front door of my kids' home day care that is a daily reminder of what raising children is all about. Joshua is speaking to the tribes of Israel when he says, "But as for me and my

Jason and Stella

household, we will serve the Lord" (Joshua 24:15). This verse is a daily reminder that keeps my Lord and Savior first in our house. It reminds me that to have godly children, I must raise them in a godly way. Without the Lord in my house, I have failed as a parent. With the Lord, all things are possible, even when I mess things up and make parental mistakes. So praise be to the God in heaven who blessed me with a beautiful wife, an incredible little boy, a precious little girl . . . and a dog.

CHAPTER 14

THE NEW FEAR

"PTSD is a whole-body tragedy, an integral human event of enor-
mous proportions with massive repercussions."

~ Susan Pease Banitt

I HAD THE MISFORTUNE OF watching a horror flick on television not too long ago. It was the typical slasher film where the hopeless teenage girl runs screaming through the woods while a homicidal maniac slowly follows after her. Of course, the girl trips and falls and, out of the blue, the killer jumps out of who-knows-where and proceeds to end her life in ways that would be inappropriate to describe in this book.

I can't say that any of these movies ever really scared me in the past, but they certainly don't scare me now. If anything, these movies are more comedies than horror. The only real horror about the movie I watched was that someone actually thought it was a good idea to make this movie. Seriously, the movie was horrific.

After you've defeated death in a stare off, the fear that you once knew no longer has the potency it once had. I remember being so scared, not only in the moment that I was shot, but before October 17, 2012. Fear is traditionally defined as being afraid of (something or someone). This kind of fear has been put on the back burner for a different kind of fear. No longer am I afraid that I might die in a warm parking lot on a fall evening. My fear is of the mental capacity.

PTSD, or post-traumatic stress disorder, has gained recognition in mainstream society in the past decade or so with the help of organizations like the Wounded Warrior Project or Navy Safe Harbor. PTSD hasn't just popped up out of nowhere but has affected humankind since the beginning of time. Thousands of years ago, an Egyptian combat veteran named Hori wrote about the feelings he experienced before going into battle: "You determine to go forward . . . shuddering seizes you, the hair on your head stands on end, your soul lies in your hand."

Our grandfathers, who earned the title "The Greatest Generation," weren't exempt from this condition either. Nightmares, heavy drinking, and flashbacks were the norm after they got back from war, effects that were swept under the rug and kept locked behind closed doors. If they felt the effects of battle, they didn't open up and talk about it to anybody. Seeing a therapist or a psychologist in those times was taboo; talking to someone about your feelings and fears was unmanly in the 40s and 50s, or so I've been told. Only when society began to open up to the idea that PTSD might be an actual condition did those soldiers, who mentally never left the front lines of battle, step forward and speak about their everyday horrors.

Merriam-Webster defines PTSD as "a psychological reaction occurring after experiencing a highly stressing event (as wartime combat, physical violence, or a natural disaster) that is usually characterized by depression, anxiety, flashbacks, recurrent nightmares, and avoidance of reminders of the event." I didn't realize I had PTSD until my Navy doctor pointed it out to me. I've always prided myself as having it all together after the incident. I made sure I was always smiling to show people that I took this tragedy and brushed it off. I wanted people to think that, because of the Lord in my life, I hadn't changed one bit. But as days turned into weeks, and weeks to months, I knew something was wrong.

It wasn't long before I decided to go and see a mental health professional. The particular therapist I see on a weekly basis specializes in PTSD and knows the signs and symptoms. After speaking with her for a few weeks, she determined what was going on in my life and how the disorder was affecting me. It took her awhile to get something out of me because I wanted everybody to see how I have my stuff together. A broken man is something I don't want people to see, but a broken man is exactly what I am.

The worst part about seeing a PTSD therapist is the homework assignments. I've had to color, paint, cut, and write my feelings. For example, my therapist gave me a white face mask and told me to decorate it however I wanted. She wanted it to be decorated with how I feel or who I think I am. The only thing I could do is keep it white. When asked, I told her that before I knew the Lord, this mask would have been black with cracks and blood dripping out, but now that Jesus has died for my sins, I'm pure, without sin. She thought I was just being lazy.

I kick and scream, but I know therapy ultimately helps me open up. Here is a paper I wrote in therapy:

AWAKENED

The heavy rain pelts my window as the sun struggles to shine its rays on the gray earth below.

How many days has it been raining?

I ask myself as I try to find a clear thought from the nightmare that I just fought my way out of.

My leg. My leg.

Such a bad dream. He was coming for me. Eyes as red as
the flames he came from. His face; his body; dragon like in
appearance yet human like as well.

Thank God it was a dream. Thank God.

Reaching down my right leg . . . Reaching my right stump . . .

My leg! MY LEG!

No dream. No nightmare. No foot.

Thunder rings out in the distance. I sit up on the side of
the bed and stare down at my new foot leaning against the
box spring.

I'm still in my dream. It's still my nightmare. I'm gonna
wake up whole again. Just wake up, Brett. Wake up, Brett!!

Nothing. The air is thick and stale in my bedroom.

Why can't I breathe? Why do I hurt? Focus, Brett. Focus!

The storm grows stronger. The wind picks up, riddling the
window with waves of rain.

Then I hear it. Shallow and quick breathing. The stench
curls into my nostrils and singes my hair as my eyes are
drawn to the dark corner of the room. I see the silhouette

of the creature with the red eyes. He's here. He's always been here. He's been waiting for this moment my whole life. Waiting to devour me, conquer me . . . break me.

Stay calm. Stay calm. Breathe. Breathe. Come on, Brett! Breathe! Wake up, Brett! Wake up! I just want to wake up! I just want to sleep! Sleep, Brett. Close your eyes and never wake up. I can't. I can't. She needs me . . . He needs me . . . She needs me.

"You'll never make it, Brett."

It speaks!

The sound of its voice brings uncontrollable shivering deep within my body. I fight to keep from crying out in sheer terror.

"Brett . . . It's ok. I'll take care of you. The sun will never come out again. Where is it? Where am I?"

He's making sense. When was the last time I've seen the sun? I can't remember the last time it wasn't raining.

"I'll never leave you, Brett. I'm right here . . . I will always be right here."

A decrepit smile curls across its face as the crackling of lightning illuminates the corner of the room, exposing spider like limbs busily touching and stroking themselves in triumph.

"I know you're hurting, Brett. Take my hand and you'll hurt no more."

I'm hurting so bad. I don't want to feel the pain anymore. I don't want to get up. I don't want to live. I just want to lie down. I want to sleep.

As it inches closer, I can smell its breath and suddenly feel nauseous.

It's death. It smells like death.

"Just close your eyes and relax. Just sleep. You deserve it. You just need to rest. I'll keep watch; you just sleep."

He's right. I'm so tired. I just need to sleep . . . I can't sleep.

The wind grows louder and the clouds grow thicker as it anticipates my next move.

I need to speak. I need to answer. I must.

My tongue feels swollen from the absence of water during the night. I clear my throat and utter a sentence that barely travels past my lips.

"There is a way that seems right to a man, but its end is the way of death."

"What did you just say? What are you mumbling? Speak up, Brett. What is your decision?"

The rain begins to die down.

Come on, Brett. Answer it. Say something!

I'm clearer this time:

"He will call on me, and I will answer him. I will be with him in trouble. I will deliver him and honor him."

The rain stops as the clouds begin to surrender to the rays of the sun, allowing them to peak through and stroke the window beside me. The creature's eyes widen as he begins to inch back into the corner.

"Brett . . ."

Keep talking, Brett. Come on.

"They will fight against you but will not overcome you, for I am with you and will rescue you, declares the Lord!"

The creature contorts its body and belts out a toe-curling scream. I want to run. I want to close my eyes. I want to hide.

Keep talking, Brett. I'm scared. Don't be afraid, man! Come on! As I walk . . .

". . . through the valley of the shadow of death, I will fear no evil, for you are with me! Your rod and your staff, they comfort me!"

The sun shoots through the window, finally breaking the gray, finally breaking the night. The light fills the dark cor-ner with light brighter than any I ever remember seeing before. The creature melts against the wall and disappears into a cloud of vapor.

It's gone.

He's come.

I'm awake.

I loved sleep. Growing up, I went to bed early and woke up late. Then when I got married, my wife wanted to stay up until eleven-thirty, but I was content with lights out at nine. After the incident, however, all changed. The only way the nurses were able to put me to sleep in the hospital was to give me some kind of sleeping pill. Unfortunately, when the drugs wore off, I awakened with a panic attack. Time and time again, I would beg for some oxygen because I couldn't breathe. I was sure that there wasn't any air in my hospital room. It was later I realized what was going on with me.

When I arrived home from my four-month stay in the hospital, two o'clock in the morning would roll around and I was still flipping through the channels. Every time I closed my eyes, I could see the gunman who tried to take my life. The same cold eyes and dark face stared at me, but in the darkness, there was a tiny yellow glow in his pupils.

When I finally fell asleep, I relived that night all over again. Sometimes, my monster (better known as the gunman) didn't run away. Instead, he stood over me while ignoring my plea for mercy and shot me five more times. In a few variations of the nightmare, I wasn't the one being shot. There were several times when it was my son lying in the shadow of the devil's right hand (aka the gun). I was off in the distance, yelling for him to spare Jason and shoot me, but he grinned, turned toward my son lying on the ground, and shot him. Other times it's my wife, family members, or close friends. Those dreams shake me up for about a month or so. Most of the time, it's just me and me alone.

The pain is another daily factor. My pain has been relived every night of my life since October 17, 2012. The kind of pain that comes from being shot to my degree should be experienced only once in a person's life. For me, the pain doesn't end when I fall asleep; it just increases.

Mornings are probably the hardest part of my days. Not only have I failed to get any sleep, but I wake up to another nightmare. One of my early childhood nightmares was that I was missing a leg. Well, waking up every morning, praying that it was all a bad dream, only to realize your nightmare is your new reality, is very taxing.

I usually start my day with reaching down my right leg to feel a cold and scar ridden stump just past my knee. Then I see my prosthetic leaning on the side of my bed, and I get angry. I'm not angry at the world or anything; I'm angry at the prosthetic, literally angry at it. I hate the fact that I have to take ten minutes out of my day to put it on. Not only is my prosthetic not my actual foot, but the first few steps cause incredible pain in my residual limb. I'm banking on my body eventually getting used to it and the pain becoming a distant memory, but I'm not sure if I'm being realistic. After a few hours, my leg feels okay, and I try and get everything done that's on my "to do" list. But, as the day closes and its bath time for the kids, my leg begins to break down. The pain gets to the point where I have to take some pain medication in order to stop obsessing about it. I want to be able to spend time with my family without the pain, a constant reminder that I don't have a leg anymore.

I didn't realize how much sudden loud noises bothered me until I was in Hawaii for the "Wounded Warrior Safe Harbor Pacific Invitational." The "WWPI" is a competition between all the military branches in events such as track & field, shot put, discus, and swimming. The first day of competition was the track & field portion. As I stated previously, I wasn't able to run yet, so I elected to compete in the discus and shot put while the other wounded warriors were getting ready to run the track events. About an hour into my stretching, they started the first track event with a gunshot. The host of the event failed to warn the warriors with PTSD (which included me). I just about had a panic attack. I wasn't the only one either. The host apologized for the communication breakdown, and the track meet continued. Needless to say, there were a bunch of shaken athletes. I was shocked at how a noise paralyzed my body. I was ashamed of how I reacted. I thought to myself, what a coward I've become. I knew irrational thinking was rearing its ugly head, but I couldn't help but feel shame.

My avoidance of crowds of people and certain places is something else that I struggle with. If I had my way, I would never leave my house. It's a scary situation for me to go out into the world with potential danger. The fact that I'm not at one-hundred percent is the most difficult for me. I know that I'm wounded, and other people see it too. If you watch National Geographic enough, you know that predators always single out the wounded animal because it's easier to catch. I can't protect my family like I need to if someone approaches. Even if I'm not with my family, if danger approaches, I can't get away anymore. Fight or flight isn't an option now. I must fight, and it must be on one leg.

The Lord must have a sense of humor. He knows what goes on in my mind, yet He chose me to go to churches, schools, and businesses to tell my story and glorify His name through it. I don't feel comfortable in front of crowds. I know few people feel great about public speaking, but my fear is more out of an "Oh gosh, someone's gonna shoot me!" feeling. I know it's an irrational fear, but it's a fear that I'm working through, and even if I always have this fear, I would still stand in front of a crowd and testify of what the Lord did in my life because this is what He's chosen me to do. I'm humbled and honored to do it. As long as the crowd doesn't stand or sit behind me, I'm not going to freak out while speaking. Then again, my God is the God who made the heavens and the earth and separated the day from the night, so I'm pretty sure He'll calm my head when it's game time.

My biggest new fear in my life keeps me up even longer at night when I think about it. It's an aesthetic fear but doesn't focus on vanity. It has to do with my children. As you may remember from previous chapters, I have two beautiful children: a little boy, Jason, and a little girl, Stella. My biggest fear is that one day they will be embarrassed by me. Not in the way that most teenagers are embarrassed by their folks, but an embarrassment due to my deformity. Children are children, this I know, and they don't think in the same capacity that most adults think in. I love my boy and sweet little girl so much. I fought to stay alive for them. To think that one day they won't want me around because I don't have a leg or have a bunch of scars makes me feel like I'm dying all over again. Will they understand what their daddy went through? Will they know why I have these scars or why I don't have a leg? Will they even care?

I know that this particular fear may be irrational, but it's a fear

nonetheless. I pray every night that my children will treat me like any other teenager treats their father. If they are embarrassed by me, let it be because of my corny jokes or the way I dress. I can take those kinds of insults, but not the ones that have to do with my sacrifice for them.

I've been diagnosed with severe PTSD, and every day has been a struggle. The good news is that this may not be a permanent fixture in my life. People learn to

Freedom helps me cope with my PTSD

cope with their sickness in an effective way every day of their lives. I know that this is going to be an everyday struggle, but I am up for the challenge. Paul wrote to the church in Philippi and told them, in Philippians 4:13, "I can do all things through Christ who gives me strength." I know that, with the Lord, I can defeat this. But until then, I will do God's will no matter the outcome.

CHAPTER 15

WAS IT WORTH IT?

There is no greater love than to lay down one's life for one's friends.

~ John 15:13 NLT

SINCE THE DAWN OF TIME, we have been fighting wars and seeing battles against good and evil. World War II, the Korean, Vietnam, and Iraqi wars have been fought because "evil" was trying to overcome "good" and it was our job as Americans to make sure that "good" always came out victorious. The question arises, "Was it worth it?" Opinions vary. Depending on who you ask, you probably get differing answers. If you ask a politician from any party affiliation, you may be told that it was definitely worth it because of the political situations in and around the world. On the other hand, parents of a fallen soldier may tell you that it was not worth it at all. I am making generalizations because there are some politicians who hate war no matter the circumstances and some parents who believed in the vision that their child was fighting for. No matter what the situation, there will be differing opinions when the question is asked. "Was it worth it?"

When I walk down the street or I'm sitting in a coffee shop, people often ask me what happened to my leg. Ironically, people typically assume one of two things. Either I lost my leg in Iraq or Afghanistan, or I was in a motorcycle accident. Once I explain how I lost my leg, people usually look at me with astonishment. Many thank me for what I did, then throw out a comment that they don't know if they could do what I did. The truth is, if I were asked before the incident if I could do something like that, I don't know what I would say. There was only one person who, after I told him the story, said that he would have done the same thing. I was a bit shocked by how sure he was of himself.

On the other end of the spectrum, a comment from a nurse floored me. She was a very sweet woman who treated me well. When I first met her, she came into my hospital room to clean my recently amputated leg. While cleaning my wounds, she asked me to tell her my story. I took about twenty minutes or so to tell her everything that happened. By the time I finished, I was exhausted and was expecting a pat on the back or a compliment for my courageous act as I had been accustomed to getting in the past. Instead, she looked at me and said, "You should've minded your own business. Now look at you." To be honest, I am not one to get my feelings hurt very easily, but this was fairly soon after I woke up from my coma, and her comment really upset me. She was basically telling me that I was stupid for helping and my condition was my entire fault. If I had only minded my own business, I would be home with my wife and kids and both feet.

Somehow the Lord put into my path a quote by Edmund Burke. He said:

All that is required for evil to prevail is for good men to do nothing.

A great dilemma is presented in this thought. If a person sees wrong and does not stand up for good, evil will win and this world is lost. On the other hand, if evil roams and a person stands up for good, there is a possibility of being harmed for the greater good of society. It is a double-edged sword.

As a result, I thought about the nurse's comment for a few weeks. The following questions rolled over and over in my mind. *Should I have minded my own business? Should I have looked away? Was it worth the pain and suffering I had been forced to endure and am still enduring to this day?* These questions were tough to answer. I'm not going to lie; I was on the fence for a while, but once I had an answer to these questions, I felt joy and complete peace in my heart.

The nurse came in a few weeks later, and I told her I had been thinking about what she said to me that day, and I had an answer for her. I said to her:

"Doing the right thing is always worth it, no matter the consequences."

It is enough to say that she was a bit shocked by my response, not because of what I said to her but because of the kind of person that she portrayed herself to be in our previous conversation. I can only speculate on what she was thinking, but it seemed that she had a change of heart after we talked.

Maybe you are of the same mindset as the nurse was in our first conversation. Since October 17, 2012, I have experienced great pain. I was shot at close range. I had fifty-one units of blood transfused into me. I lost thirteen liters of blood in the first twenty-four hours after the incident. I lost a kidney, a third of my colon, and had my right leg amputated below the knee. I had over a dozen surgeries in two weeks and about five more to correct other issues as a result of my injuries. Because of all the surgeries, I now have lymphedema in my left leg and suffer from severe PTSD. I have daily stump pain, phantom pain, and abdominal pain that are barely masked with strong pain killers.

Let's look at the other end of the spectrum. I have a beautiful wife with a heart of gold who loves me dearly. I get to spend the rest of my days growing old with her. I am able to see my son grow up and, more importantly, my son will grow up with a father. Not just any father, but a father who risked his life to right a wrong. My sweet little Stella has been born into this world, and now she has her daddy. I have the chance to hold her in my arms and look into her eyes. I now have the chance to walk her down the aisle on her wedding day and take the first dance with her. She too has a "hero" in her father. I have started to lay the foundation of a legacy both of my children will be proud of.

The result I am proud of the most is the opportunity to tell others about the Lord and what He has done in my life. Before October 17, 2012, I was a man who pretty much had it all together. However, if I walked in front of a group of people and started telling them about God, I assume they would look at me and think to themselves, "Who's this guy? He's never gone through anything! He doesn't understand what I'm going through!"

As a result of the tragedy I suffered, I have credibility that I didn't have before. I have had so much happen to me that the average person would not blame me if I turned away from God. The fact that I praise Him even more than before is puzzling, to say the least. My attitude toward life and our Creator makes people turn inward and ask themselves if they would make the same decision I had made and, if so, would they still have a loving and deep relationship with the Lord, or would it be a resenting and absent relationship.

I am not trying to make light of any person's situation. I have seen and talked to many people who are going through a season of their life that I could not even imagine going through. Now I have a story that will encourage others as they go through troubled times. My story epitomizes how God can take a tragedy and turn it into an opportunity to glorify Him.

I have to be honest and reveal something that really disturbs me. I talk to people all over America and discuss things that are going on in their lives. It is natural for Christians and non-Christians to tell me how they are suffering, both physically and emotionally. Probably out of guilt, some will stop in mid-sentence, and say, "I don't know why I'm telling you this. This is nothing compared to what you went through." Let me explain why this is upsetting to me.

Everybody has problems. My problem may be worse than yours, but guess what; there are people in this world who have far greater problems than I do. It doesn't mean I'm not hurting, and at the same time, it doesn't mean you're not hurting. We all have our own crosses to bear. The good news is that God doesn't put more on your plate than you and He together can handle. If you feel like He's given you too much, you're underestimating Him. Our Lord has given you just enough to mold you into the person He wants you to be. I heard it said once that we wouldn't appreciate the sun without the rain, and I agree with that whole heartedly.

When I look at what happened in my life, I don't feel upset because my life was turned upside down. I feel honored. It sounds a bit silly, but I feel honored the Lord trusted me with this situation. God trusted me enough to say I can handle this responsibility. He knew I wouldn't curse His name or ask Him "why" when it came to my pain and suffering. The bottom line is this: if I had gotten shot and lost everything and never saw any miracles or heard God speaking to and through me, that would have been fine . . . because His grace is sufficient for me. The fact that through His Son, Jesus, my sins have been forgiven and I can live in heaven with Him for eternity is all that matters. But He has allowed me the humbling task of standing in front of people and writing books to tell of His glory. That is a great bonus in my life.

We are all broken and scarred in one way or another. My scars are physical. When you look at me, you can see that I'm broken. But some scars are not visible. Some of us are broken physically, and others are broken emotionally. Still others are broken spiritually. There is great news for all of us. We can all experience a miracle! My brother's pastor, Dr. Don Wilton, says that a miracle is something that only God can do. The miracle offered to each one of us is that God loved us so much, He sent his Son to die on the cross for our sins so we could have a second shot to spend eternity in heaven. This is our only way to spend forever in paradise. God could have easily told us we only had one shot and lost it with Adam and Eve's sin of disobedience. But He chose to give us another chance and, if we only turn to Jesus, our sins are forgiven.

So, after reassessing all the trauma, pain, fear, and brokenness, I've come to the same conclusion that I gave the nurse some months ago. Yes, it was worth it. Doing the right thing is always worth it, no matter the consequence. As far as my life goes, the perfection I thought my life was before pales in comparison to the perfection my life is now.

It is amazing when I look back at my life and see how much God was involved in the details. For such a long time, I thought that I might not have a purpose here on Earth. I think, at one time or another, we all might feel a sense of meaninglessness. But looking back, I see that the Lord was preparing me for my purpose.

From the early morning wrestling shows as a child to coaching football as an adult, I was being groomed for something greater. It's sad that I didn't trust the Lord and realize He was refining me for greater things. I didn't trust that He was preparing an incredible journey ahead of me. If I had looked at all these seemingly meaningless tasks as preparation for God's great adventure plan in my life, I would have lived a fuller life. It is the same for you. God has a purpose for you too. I know you might not think so, but it's true. If you don't believe what you're reading, open up the Word of God; open up the Bible and there you'll find in Psalm 139 that He has a purpose specifically for your life.

Take a quick assessment of your character. Do the words integrity, honesty, caring for others, love, forgiveness, and being more like Jesus come to mind? If not, there's a problem. God has a certain character in mind for us to develop to stand with Him and spread His message throughout. You see, if we become whom God wants us to be, then He will charge us with a task that only we can do to accomplish His purpose. In essence, our purpose is to accomplish His purpose. This applies to my life, but applies to yours as well.

Much easier said than done, I know. As I am writing this, there are still issues that I haven't totally taken care of. I would love to sit back and tell you I exemplify all the fruits of the spirit and have complete trust in the Lord, but I would be lying. After all God has done for me, taking an impossible situation and making it possible, I still struggle to trust Him.

My son has recently been diagnosed with Chiari Malformation. Chiari is fairly common. It's basically a condition where brain tissue extends into the spinal cord and could, if not treated, cause permanent damage to the spinal cord. As a result, Jason has to have brain surgery. Just thinking about it brings tears to my eyes. I'm scared for my son. I'm afraid of what might happen. What if something goes wrong? What if I lose him?

I can't believe what I think sometimes. Our God and Savior, the One who made the mountains and told the oceans that they can come this far but no farther, is in control of all things. He is the One who took a weak gunshot victim who had only a .001% chance of breathing seven hours later and allowed him not only to survive but to thrive in his new life. Here I am, worried that my son won't be all right. I've had face-to-face contact with the Lord and know that I know that I know that I know He is the protector and healer, but I still worry about my son's well being. But this is the story of our humanity, isn't it? Especially these days, trust is hard to embrace but is a necessity to live for God's purpose. This is an everyday struggle for me, and I suspect it may be for you as well. I constantly remind myself of the following: "I once was lost, but now I am found. I once was blind, but now I see." The Lord's love covers my soul and, if you let Him, He will cover yours as well. The same God who yelled into the tomb, "Lazarus, come out!" is in our corner. The same Lord who was nailed to a tree, was buried, and rose three days later knows every hair on our heads. If we just surrender all and put our trust in Him, our lives will be full and purposeful.

As I end this chapter, I must share with you a very important piece of my journey. The man who shot me tried to take everything from me. One second I had everything I could possibly want in this world, and the next second, because this person didn't want to get caught in his crime, he tried to take my life and with it, all that I held most dear.

If I were to tell you that I have a deep hatred toward him because of what he did to me, you probably wouldn't blame me. But I don't. Even though it's natural for us to hold grudges and ill will toward those who do or attempt to do us harm, I don't. Forgiveness isn't the first thing you may think, but I do. Some may even be offended by the word forgiveness when it comes to this attempted murderer. But how could we deny forgiveness to a person when we ourselves have been forgiven for taking the life of Jesus? Jesus was nailed to the cross by me and the sins in my life. The wounds on His back were a result of the beating He received for our sins. We spat in His face and hurled insults at Him as He died on the cross, yet He forgave us. He not only forgave us, but He loves us and stands in our corner at the gates of heaven when we stand to be judged. If we acknowledge His royalty over the heavens and the earth and repent, He will forgive our sins.

My shooter will stand trial in the next couple of months, and I will be called to testify against him. I will do so and let the jury find a verdict. If he is found guilty, my plan is to go and visit him. Not to find understanding or even to try and get an apology out of him. I will go visit him to ask if there is anything he needs. I have forgiven this man, although it wasn't easy to do. But because of the Lord's strength, I have no anger toward him. He needs Jesus just like I do. He needs salvation, just like me. So I will show Jesus to him. I will ask him if there is anything he needs. If he won't see me, I'll leave, but I'll be back next month and ask the same thing. He needs to know that there is a greater love out there, and it doesn't come from me or any other person alive today. This love comes from our Lord and Savior Jesus Christ, and He forgives our sins. He forgave me, and He will forgive him too. In light of this, who am I not to forgive this man who shot me? The Bible says, "Forgive, and you shall be forgiven." The Bible doesn't say, "Forgive if you feel like it, and you will be forgiven."

CHAPTER 16

THE KING AND I

I know the LORD is always with me. I will not be shaken, for he
is right beside me.

~ Psalms 16:8 NLT

I'M FINISHING THIS BOOK WITH a chapter that I feel I need to write. A few of the other chapters in this book have been pretty difficult for me because of having to rehash memories in my recent past, but writing this chapter is a breeze. This chapter is easy for me because it deals with the greatest decision that I've ever made in my life, and that's my decision to follow Jesus Christ all of my days.

At the early age of seven (or was it eight), palms sweaty and knees shaky, I walked down the aisle at my church in Miami and told the pastor I wanted to accept Jesus into my heart. I realized that I was a sinner and that the only way to heaven was to believe that God sent His only Son (Jesus Christ) to die on the cross for my sins.

You see, before Jesus, God's one and only Son, was born onto the earth, the Jews had to sacrifice an animal to atone for their sins. The Jewish man would take a lamb, hold a ceremony where he would symbolically place all his sins onto the animal, and sacrifice it. They would have to do this annually because they would sin on a daily basis. If they were to die before they could sacrifice a lamb, they would be unclean with sin and would not get into the kingdom of heaven. But God made the chosen people a promise that He would send His only Son to be the ultimate sacrifice. God's Son would be the sacrificial lamb that would take everybody's sin—past, present, and future—and pay the penalty for all those sins with His life so that whoever would believe in the sacrificial lamb would not perish, but have eternal life in heaven. John 3:16 says it clearly.

For God so loved the world that he gave his one and only Son,
that whoever believes in him shall not perish but have eternal life.

But at the age of seven (or eight), I didn't know all of this. I just knew that I wasn't perfect; I sin. And the only way to get to heaven—and stay out of hell—was to accept Jesus into my heart. So the pastor crouched down to my level and asked if we could pray together. We bowed our heads, and he asked me to repeat after him.

"Jesus, I know that I am a sinner, and I ask for your forgiveness. I believe you died for my sins and rose from the dead.
I turn from my sins and invite you to come into my heart
and life. I want to trust and follow you as my Lord and
Savior. In your name, amen."

When I opened my eyes, I felt a sense of liberation. The pastor threw his arms around me and told me that I had made the most important decision that I'd ever make in my life. A few weeks later, I was baptized. I was officially a Christian, but I didn't truly understand what it meant until I got a little older . . . like eight years older.

Since I had asked Jesus into my heart, the Lord had been doing a good work in me. He had been refining me and molding me into the kind of man He wanted me to be. But I was fighting Him all the way. I was a fan of the things of this world. Sometimes I would give in to peer pressure or temptation, and I would explain it away and justify it somehow. I would open the Bible and read Romans 3:23 that says, "For all have sinned and fall short of the glory of God." I would read that and say, "See! We all sin. It's cool! That is why I have Jesus." But, if I continued reading Romans, I would see that having Jesus in our lives doesn't give us license to do what we want; on the contrary, we represent something far greater than ourselves now. I didn't understand this until later in high school and into college.

In high school, I would go to a church camp or a youth choir tour and come back so excited to have a relationship with the Lord. I wanted to tell everybody about God and what He had done in my life and what He could do in their lives. I was "on fire" for the Lord. But, in time, the raging fire would turn into glowing embers. I never really understood why this happened to me. I wasn't oblivious to the situation. I knew when I was falling away. I knew when my daily Christian routine was just a daily Christian routine. I became dried up, empty.

Then October 17 came rolling along, and my life would never be the same again. A single bullet ripped through my stomach and sent me as close to death as any man could be without actually dying, and that made me more alive than ever. Both my physical life as well as my spiritual life were forever changed. This was the day I realized why I seemed to have been on a spiritual "roller coaster" ride. Before I got shot, God was always a distant God in my eyes. He was always up in the clouds, sitting on a comfy chair, wagging His finger at me as I groveled here on Earth. I would pray to Him and talk to Him, but I would always look up. He was sitting high on His throne, and I was down in the depths, eating the rinds that were being fed to the pigs like in the story of The Prodigal Son. Then I was shot. As I was dying, I asked God to help me. I told the Lord I needed Him at that moment. And He was no longer sitting high on His throne. He was no longer up there in His comfy chair. He was right beside me, holding me. The Lord took His mighty hand and held the wound tight so I wouldn't bleed out. The Lord took His other hand and laid it on my back, comforting me. I felt Him. He was right beside me. And then it hit me. He had always been right beside me. Ever since I prayed the prayer of salvation when I was seven (or eight), He's been walking with me, and He was with me in my moment of greatest need. What is so encouraging is I know He's with me right now. Psalm 23 describes it clearly:

> The Lord is my shepherd, I lack nothing.

> He makes me lie down in green pastures, he leads me beside quiet waters,

> He refreshes my soul. He guides me along the right paths for his name's sake.

> Even though I walk through the darkest valley, I will fear no evil, for you are with me; your rod and your staff, they comfort me.

You prepare a table before me in the presence of my enemies. You anoint my head with oil; my cup overflows.

Surely your goodness and love will follow me all the days of my life, and I will dwell in the house of the Lord forever.

Even though I walk through the valley of the shadow of death (some translations say), God is with me. His goodness and love will follow me all the days of my life. Notice it says "will." It doesn't say His goodness and love *might* follow me or *used* to follow me; it says *will* follow me. I take such courage in what the Lord promises.

There is a story in the Bible that reminds me of my life. It's found in Luke fifteen. It's the story of the lost son. Jesus tells a story about a man with two sons.

The younger son went to his father and said he wanted his half of his inheritance. His father said okay and divided the land and belongings between the two sons. The youngest son gathered everything that was given to him and left the household. He went off into a distant land and spent his days and nights essentially partying.

Well, when you party as hard as he partied, you don't have time to work, so he spent all his inheritance. Just his luck, right after he spent all his money, there was a severe famine. The whole country was in need, so he decided to get any job that he could get. After awhile, he got a job from one of the citizens of the country who had him feeding the pigs on his land. Now, this is as low as you can get for a Jewish man. The Jews in that day believed that pigs were unclean, and they wouldn't eat, touch, or feed them. He was so hungry that the pig's food looked good to him and he longed to "fill his stomach with the pods that the pigs were consuming," but no one gave him any food.

He thought back to his father at home and his father's workers and knew they were well taken care of. He decided he would go back home with bowed head and ask his father for a job. He wanted to work in his father's fields so that he wouldn't go hungry anymore. On the way home, he was preparing what he was going to say to his father. As he walked over the hillside, his father spotted him. As soon as that father spotted his son, he dropped everything and ran to him. When he got to his son, he threw his arms around him and kissed him. He told his servants to bring his son the best robe and the family ring and put them on him. The father also ordered his servants to kill the fattened calf and prepare to celebrate with a feast. Then, in Luke 15:24, the father says, "For this son of mine was dead and is alive again; he was lost and is found."

This is an illustration of God's love for us. By the way, this is the only time in the Bible that God runs. If you'd like to read this story in more detail, it's found in Luke 15:11–32. This story rings so true to me. When I was shot, I was as low as low could be. I was feeding pigs and longing to fill my stomach with the pods that the pigs were eating! I was lying face down in the parking lot, fighting for my next breath and longing for it. I asked the Lord to help me and not only did He help, but He ran to me! He ran and threw His arms around me and kissed my cheek! First Peter 5:7 say the Lord cares for you. He's not some god sitting up in the clouds with a giant magnifying glass, burning us like little ants. He cares for us. And when we call, He runs to our side.

So where am I now with my King? The Lord is as essential to me as oxygen. I could not have made it through those dark times without the strength and comfort that comes from the Lord. I could not wake up every day and face my new normal without my God. Every day, I hope I'm waking up from a nightmare, only to wake up to a nightmare. I wouldn't be able to get out of bed. I wouldn't be able to live anymore. But because of my Lord and Savior Jesus Christ, all things are possible (Matthew 19:26). I know I can do anything through Jesus because He gives me strength (Philippians 4:13).

I don't know who you are. I don't know what caused you to pick up this book. The great thing is I don't have to know, you don't even have to know, but God knows. Do you know that God knew you before you were born? If you have never heard or wanted to hear about this God stuff, I hope you aren't offended. I'm here to tell my story and glorify the one who saved me that fateful day. If you are reading this book and want to know the joy that I as well as many others have experienced through our relationship with Christ, pray the prayer of salvation. You don't have to pray it word for word; it's really just a guideline to repentance. The important thing is you realize you're not living the way our Creator intended and you want to change who you are, through Christ Jesus.

As for me and my relationship with the King, Jesus Christ:

I gave my life to serving our Lord and Savior, Jesus Christ when I was seven (or eight) years old. At the moment I asked God to change my heart and forgive me for my sins, my name was written in the Book of Life; I was going to heaven. I have done great things that have help introduce people to the Lord, and I've done some bad things that may have turned people away from the Lord. I know that if I were to have died that fateful night on October 17, 2012, I would have gone to heaven. I know this because of the decision that I made years ago. But would I have reached my full potential as a follower of Jesus Christ? I fear that, had I died that night and gone to heaven and come face to face with the One who took my sins from me and allowed Himself to be nailed to the cross in my place, He might have said to me, "Brett, what happened? I gave you so many opportunities to serve me and glorify my name, but you didn't do it. I gave you so many gifts and talents to use in my name, but you didn't use them for me. You could have done better. What happened?"

Would I have gone to heaven? Absolutely! Would I spend eternity with my Creator and loved ones that were also followers of Jesus Christ? No doubt! But the first meeting between Jesus and me wouldn't have been as joyous as it could be. Joyous? Yes. But as joyous as it could be? Probably not.

But I survived. Nobody knows how I made it through. The doctors are even baffled. But our God is a God who moves mountains. Our God, who knew my name before the heavens and earth were even created, chose to save me, chose to move mountains in my own life. He chose me for something greater. A foolish man would survive a fatal ordeal like this and say, "Thanks, God, but no thanks!" and go off and do his own thing. A wise man would recognize what the Lord has done for him and do everything he could to let all know that the Lord, who made him out of dust, snatched him out of the hands of death and made him feel more alive than ever. I am the latter of the two.

He has saved my life for a reason. I shouldn't be here, and I know it. I'm living on borrowed time. I will do all that I can to tell my story and glorify God through it. I know when I stand before the Lord, I'll be standing alone. This journey I'm on right now is my own. So I will live and breathe for my King, Jesus Christ. And when Jesus and I meet face to face in the future, I hope He throws open His arms with a big smile on His face, holds me tight, and says to me, "Well done, good and faithful servant!" Amen.

Representing the USA in London at the Invictus Games

ABOUT THE AUTHOR

On October 17, 2012, Brett Parks was shot in the abdomen while breaking up a robbery. Because of his injuries, Brett spent 20 days in a coma. Upon waking, Brett found that he had lost a kidney, a third of his colon, and the lower part of his right leg.

Brett is the founder and president of Second Shot Ministry and travels around the nation speaking to schools, businesses, and churches about hope, faith, and how he overcame a 99.999% mortality rate.

Because of his heroic actions, Brett was rewarded with the governor's Medal of Merit, which was presented by Governor Rick Scott.

The city of Jacksonville also acknowledged Brett by presenting him with a proclamation stating that December 5th is Brett Parks Day.

When Brett is not traveling, he loves spending time with his beautiful wife Susan and playing with his son Jason and daughter Stella.

For booking, go to:
www.secondshotministry.com
@SecondShotCom

For more information about

Brett Parks

&

Miracle Man

please visit:

www.secondshotministry.com
@SecondShotCom

....

For more information about
AMBASSADOR INTERNATIONAL
please visit:

www.ambassador-international.com
@AmbassadorIntl
www.facebook.com/AmbassadorIntl